ECHOES OF DETROIT

A 300-YEAR HISTORY

IRWIN COHEN

Map courtesy of Ste. Anne de Detroit

Printed in the United States of America

05 04 03 02 01   5 4 3 2

ISBN 0-9677570-0-2

Published by City Vision Publishing
in cooperation with Boreal Press, Inc.
1629 Haslett Road, Suite 178
Haslett, Michigan 48840 USA

COVER PHOTOS AND ILLUSTRATIONS

Front cover, top left: 1962 street scene of Campus Martius by Harry Wolf.
Bottom: Aerial view of Comerica Park and Detroit skyline courtesy of Michigan Views.

Back cover, top: National Theater and the Monroe Block, 1910, courtesy of Michigan Views.
Bottom: Riverfront area on Detroit's 300th birthday, July 24, 2001, photo by the author.

Things were primitive at best in early Detroit. The Indians weren't always friendly with the settlers, nor with other tribes. Some Indians circulated false rumors, trying to stir up trouble between tribes loyal to the French.

The rumors resulted in an attack on the post in which Cadillac's house, Ste. Anne's Church, and the residence of the priest were burned and destroyed in 1703. Enough peace was restored to rebuild and the following year a daughter was born to the Cadillacs—the first white child born in Detroit.

In 1706, while Cadillac was in Montreal trying to recruit new settlers for Detroit, a dog belonging to the temporary commander bit an Ottawa brave in the leg. The Indian kicked the animal and Commander de Bourgmont retaliated by beating the Indian so severely that he died soon after.

The angered Ottawas avenged the death by attacking the Miamis, the favorite tribe of the French. The Miamis retreated into the stockade while the 15 soldiers in the fort fired on the Ottawas, killing several, but not before a priest was killed trying to find safety in the fort.

Time and the return of Cadillac cooled tempers

Three centuries ago the small waterfront covered the area of what is now the Civic Center. (IC/DHM)

The same area three centuries later. (IC)

and an uneasy peace reigned. Newly arrived settlers were given small house lots within the fort and were allowed to farm outside the fort. The farm grants were known as ribbon farms, as they were from 200 to up to a thousand feet wide and extended back two or three miles. The boundaries of the farms bear the names of the original grantees: Beaubien, Campau, Chene, Livernois, Riopelle, and St. Aubin.

Detroit's residents needed permission from Cadillac to engage in any kind of trade and had to pay a tax besides. Cadillac grew rich by overcharging and overtaxing. He also kept a padlock on the imported brandy, claiming it was to protect the people from drunkeness. However, Cadillac sold the brandy to the Indians at twice the going rate.

Count Pontchartrain heard about Cadillac's greedy behavior and sent his old friend a letter expressing his disappointment. The eventual result was that Cadillac was promoted to governor of the Louisiana Territory in 1711, where he stayed for nine years before returning to France.

After Cadillac left, soldiers and settlers, aided by Huron and Ottawa Indians, put down a bloody battle with the Fox tribe. The little village of Detroit declined as few new residents arrived and some settlers who came with Cadillac left. Trade dropped off and the stockade was in need of repair. It wasn't until close to 1730 that things turned around. French wars with Great Britian made France realize that the little outpost of Detroit should be beefed up against English encroachment.

Detroit experienced slow growth and mostly peace. There was another Indian attack in 1746 that resulted in 150 soldiers arriving from Montreal the following year. More immigrants arrived in 1749 and the stockade was enlarged again. After the garrison was increased in 1751, the post took the name of Fort du Detroit.

Ste. Anne's Church (right foreground) was Detroit's dominant structure in the 1700s. (IC/DHM)

Part of the same area now. (IC)

Cadillac was booted upstairs in 1711. (IC)

The soldiers of the 1750s weren't confined to barracks. Upon enlistment they were given a small tract of land outside the fort where they could build a small home and cultivate a garden. But it was a lonely life, as very few women wanted to leave Montreal, where it was advertised that Detroit had many potential husbands. Consequently, soldiers hung around Indian camps and wedded Indian maidens.

In 1760, after fifty-nine years of French rule, Detroit was given to the British as part of the agreement of the French and Indian war. On November, 29, 1760, the British flag was raised in Detroit. Close to 600 Detroiters of French heritage lived in the area, half within the stockade and others on farms on both sides of the river.

While the population included Indians, French and British, the first German settler in Michigan took up farming in Grosse Pointe in 1751, and the first Jew to set foot in Detroit was Chapman Abraham in 1762. Abraham had varied business interests as he traded in wine, brandy, muskets, gunpowder, ball and shot, and bought and sold land. Abraham returned to Montreal later in 1762 to bring back more goods to trade and sell.

Pontiac, chief of the Ottawas, traveled long distances pow-wowing with the Chippewas, Shawnees, Delawares, Miamis, Potawatomis and Hurons, trying to unite the tribes to rid the Detroit area of whites. By the spring of 1763, Pontiac was ready for war. According to his plan, at a prescribed time, each tribe would attack simultaneously so the English would be unable to help each other.

Pontiac's plan included a surprise attack on the British inside the fort. He requested a meeting with the commanding officer, Major Henry Gladwin, that would be attended by a delegation of 60 tribal chiefs. Pontiac planned to size up the situation inside the fort while speaking to Gladwin, and, if conditions were right, give the signal for attack.

Gladwin knew of Pontiac's plan and when he thought that Pontiac gave the signal, British troops drew their swords and beat their drums. Gladwin warned Pontiac that any violence would be dealt with at once. Gladwin also assured the Indians that friendship would be extended as long as they acted peacefully.

The next day, Sunday, May 8, 1763, Pontiac and several tribal heads galloped to the fort bringing a pipe of peace. However, while Pontiac talked of peace he thought of war. Two days later the treacherous Pontiac began a siege of the fort and directed savage attacks elsewhere.

Finally, British reinforcements arrived, bringing 60 soldiers along with ammunition and provisions. Three days later on July 3, those inside the fort heard about the Peace of Paris ending the French and Indian War. Canada and Nova Scotia were ceded to the British and the French were expelled from North America.

However, Detroit had its own war to worry about, and Major Gladwin fought back by sending boats down the river and firing into Indian villages. Finally, the Potawatomies and Wyandottes tired of the killing, returned their captives, and peace was made with the two tribes.

Soon afterward, 22 barges with 280 more men, ammunition and provisions under Captain Dalyell arrived. Dalyell proposed a plan of taking large numbers of ground soldiers and staging attacks at night. Gladwin opposed the plan but reluctantly agreed.

Dalyell's surprise attack was no surprise to

Pontiac as the buzz in the fort included the time and route the English soldiers would take. A French settler or two who had no love for the English informed the Ottawa chief, and Pontiac and his braves were waiting in ambush near a narrow wooden bridge over Parent's Creek, a little south of the River Road.

On July 31 at two in the morning, Captain Dalyell took 247 men in three detachments and marched up the River Road—now Jefferson Avenue. Most of the soldiers and Captain Dalyell were slaughtered. Only 90 of the 247 men survived. So many dead and dying soldiers fell into the creek that the water turned red. From then on, that area at Jefferson and Adair was called Bloody Run.

The siege of the fort continued after the slaughter at Bloody Run for three more months without anything decisive happening. The Indians tired of it and some of the tribes left. Pontiac, however, and a few other tribes held on. Finally, Pontiac heard of the Treaty of Paris and realized that France would not regain the upper hand in the Detroit area. He lifted the siege on the last day of October 1763 and peace returned.

Peace reigned for 12 years until 1775. During the Revolutionary War, Detroit served as a base for Indian war parties, which attacked American villages near Detroit, Kentucky, Pennsylvania and New York. This time the British and Indians were on the same side.

Frontiersman Daniel Boone was captured by the Indians in Ohio as he was blazing a trail from Kentucky. Boone was brought to Detroit and imprisoned. British commander Henry Hamilton tried to ransom Boone from the Indians but they wouldn't sell Boone because of his fame and took him to one of their villages in Ohio. Boone eventually escaped, made it back to his Kentucky home, and lived for another 43 years until the ripe old age of 86.

In 1778 the British commanding officer of Detroit was Major R.B. Lernoult. He had another fort built north of the previous one at what is now the intersection of Fort and Shelby and named it after himself. Four years later the Revolutionary War was still raging but the tide was turning against the British, who still controlled Detroit and its population of 2,191, not counting the more than 500 prisoners captured mostly by the Indians and brought to the fort.

On September 3, 1783, the Treaty of Paris, the final treaty closing the war between Great Britian and the United States, was signed. The treaty recognized the independence of the United States with the Mississippi River as its western boundary.

Even though Detroit was awarded to the United States in 1783, the British refused to leave. Finally, ten years later in 1793, president George Washington decided to force a settlement and sent troops under the command of General Anthony Wayne.

The Players, founded in 1911, opened this playhouse on Jefferson in 1926. Pontiac and his braves ambushed British soldiers near this site in July 1763. (IC)

The historical marker for Fort Lernoult on the side of the Comerica Bank building at Fort and Shelby. (IC/DHM)

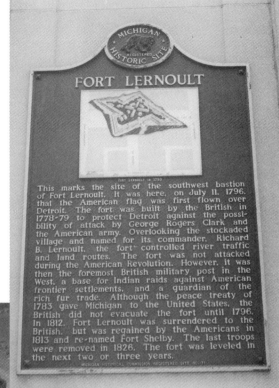

FORT LERNOULT

Fort Lernoult in 1790

This marks the site of the southwest bastion of Fort Lernoult. It was here, on July 11, 1796, that the American flag was first flown over Detroit. The fort was built by the British in 1778-79 to protect Detroit against the possibility of attack by George Rogers Clark and the American army. Overlooking the stockaded village and named for its commander, Richard B. Lernoult, the fort controlled river traffic and land routes. The fort was not attacked during the American Revolution. However, it was then the foremost British military post in the West, a base for Indian raids against American frontier settlements, and a guardian of the rich fur trade. Although the peace treaty of 1783 gave Michigan to the United States, the British did not evacuate the fort until 1796. In 1812, Fort Lernoult was surrendered to the British, but was regained by the Americans in 1813 and re-named Fort Shelby. The last troops were removed in 1826. The fort was leveled in the next two or three years.

MICHIGAN HISTORICAL COMMISSION REGISTERED SITE NO. 77

Fort Lernoult became Fort Shelby and later the corner of Fort and Shelby. (IC/DHM)

Corinthian columns and pilasters grace Comerica Bank at Fort and Shelby. The historical marker for Fort Lernoult is on the Shelby wall just off Fort. The Albert Kahn designed structure was built in 1915 and enlarged in 1926. (IC)

Called Mad Anthony Wayne because he so carefully and meticulously trained his troops for two years until he thought they were ready for battle, Wayne also confused the Indians by not advancing forward. At times he would go backward and build forts to use as refuge for advancing or retreating troops before reaching Detroit.

During this period, many Detroit homeowners and businesses had slaves. Most were captured during Indian raids in the Revolutionary War down South and brought to Michigan. In those raids, whites were massacred and blacks were exchanged for guns, ammunition and liquor. However, the slaves in Detroit were generally treated much better than those down South and some even received some type of education.

Joseph Campau owned 10 slaves, one of whom was his master's clerk and earned the respect of Detroiters for his integrity and business smarts. Other slaveowners also put some of their slaves in charge of business activities.

The British finally left Detroit in the spring of 1796 and crossed the river into Canada. On July 11, the flag of the United States flew over Detroit for the first time. Two days later, Colonel John Francis Hamtramck arrived and took command with a garrison of 300 soldiers.

In the Detroit of Hamtramck, the main gate of the stockade was present-day Cass at Jefferson. The east gate was at Griswold and that marked the outer limits of the town.

General Anthony Wayne reached Detroit on August 13, 1796, and established army headquarters. Two days later, parts of Michigan and parts of Ohio, Indiana and Wisconsin were named Wayne County in honor of General Wayne. Ninety-seven years after Cadillac landed, the big industries in town were still hunting and fishing. Half the population was French and spoke little English. One of the new arrivals was Father Gabriel Richard, who came with the title of assistant priest of St. Anne's Church.

Above: This tablet is on an exterior wall of the old County Building in Cadillac Square. (IC)

Right: The seal of Wayne County can be found on the Woodward side of the City County Building. (IC)

Father Gabriel Richard came to America from France in 1792. (IC)

THE EARLY 1800s

"A stockade encloses the town, fort and citadel. The pickets, as well as the public houses, are in a state of gradual decay and, in a few years, without repairs, must fall to the ground. The streets are narrow, straight, regular and intersect each other at right angles. The houses are, for the most part, low and inelegant."
— Charles Jouett writing about Detroit in 1803

Four years after the arrival of Father Gabriel Richard, the town of Detroit was incorporated in 1802. The northern limit was about where Warren Avenue is today. Each resident had to pay a city tax of 25 cents, and property was taxed at a rate of a quarter of 1 percent.

The following year, the respected John Frederick Hamtramck, the first American commander of Detroit, died at the age of 45. Hamtramck bought a farm east of the city and when townships were laid out, one was named for him. Ultimately, most of Hamtramck township was absorbed by Detroit, but

The official seal of the City of Detroit commemorates the great fire of 1805. The woman on the left is weeping over the loss, while the woman on the right is comforting her. The Latin words translate, "We hope for better things...it shall arise from the ashes." (IC)

the northern section still exists today as a separate city.

Detroit had a post office of its own in 1803 and Frederick Bates was the first postmaster. Not many people in town could read or write, and mail only arrived a couple of times a year from few locations.

In 1804, Detroiters were told to stay indoors at night as an Indian attack was feared. It was an uneasy time as the gates of the stockade were kept closed and guarded after dark. Watchmen patrolled the streets and a curfew was in effect. Indians weren't allowed in town after sundown, and all lanterns had to be out by 11 p.m.

The attack never materialized but Detroit would indeed be destroyed the following year. On June 11, 1805, six months after the territory of Michigan was created out of the Indiana territory with Detroit its seat of government, a baker's employee hitched his horse to a two-wheeled cart. Sparks from the man's pipe somehow connected to the hay inside the stable located where the Pontchartrain Hotel stands today. The fire spread quicker than the efforts of Detroit's residents to extinguish it.

Tears flowed as the fire cackled and residents watched their homes and town being destroyed. Many thatched buildings—some a century old and laden with memories—were reduced to ashes. All but one of Detroit's 300 buildings were destroyed. The city's 600 citizens and their animals fled to the river for safety.

Father Gabriel Richard organized the gathering of food and clothing for the homeless. As he looked at the heartbreaking scene, he was heard to murmur, *"Speramus meliora; resurget cineribus"* (we hope for better things; it will arise from its ashes). Years

The great fire of 1805 started around the corner from this site on Shelby near Jefferson. (IC)

later the Latin words uttered by Father Richard were incorporated into the official seal of the city.

The same year, U.S. President Thomas Jefferson appointed men to go to Detroit and administer the area. Men by the name of Griswold, Bates and Woodward came to govern.

Judge Augustus Woodward was in charge of deciding how Detroit would be rebuilt. Woodward was living in Washington, D.C. when the capitol was laid out. He decided that Detroit should have a similar system of interlocking hexagons and that more space should be allotted for houses and buildings. The city grew faster than the plan of hexagon streets could be implemented, but some downtown streets still remain as a reminder of Judge Woodward's plans.

Augustus Woodward was born in New York in 1774. His first name was Elias but he renamed himself Augustus as he loved Greek and Roman history.

Judge Augustus Woodward planned and named many of Detroit's streets, including Woodward Avenue.

Woodward moved to Virginia and eventually Washington to be close to his idol, Thomas Jefferson. He sold real estate and practiced law while being a Jefferson groupie, which helped him gain an appointment as one of three territorial judges of Michigan.

Tall, gaunt and pale, Woodward, who soon earned a reputation as a man who loved to drink and hated to bathe, arrived two days before the new governor, William Hull. By the time Hull arrived, Woodward was the total boss and remained almost the dictator of Detroit until he was jeered out of town after a big celebration 19 years later.

Woodward figured the most important street in town would be the one running parallel to the river, so he named it after the man who gave him the cushy job in Detroit—Jefferson. Later he honored Madison and Monroe by naming streets after them, and two minor cross streets were named after his judicial associates, Sibley and Witherell. In 1806 he gave the public square the name Campus Martius, which means military camp. People accused the egotistical Woodward of naming Detroit's main street after himself. Woodward defended himself by claiming he named the street Woodward because it traveled toward the woods.

In 1807, Governor Hull built a new stockade and a new home for himself. It was the first brick home in the city and was located at the southeast corner of Jefferson and Randolph. Today the site is part of General Motors World Headquarters.

While Woodward was one of the least popular men in town, Father Gabriel Richard was one of the most popular. The Catholic priest arranged for an organ to be brought from the east over wilderness trails. It was the first pipe organ ever heard in Detroit and was popular with the Indians, too. The curious Indians once stole the pipes to see where the sounds were coming from.

Richard was a busy man. In 1809, he started four schools, two for girls and two for boys, as well as a small, four-page newspaper. Richard's popularity with non-Catholics was such that he was asked to deliver nondenominational sermons, as there wasn't a Protestant church in town yet.

In 1811 it took 40 days to receive a letter from Washington, one of the few places from which a Detroiter could get mail. Men on horseback and men on foot navigated the long route.

In 1812 the second war with England was on, and two months after the war started, Governor Hull surrendered Detroit without firing a single shot in its defense. When British troops advanced toward Detroit and reached the area of what is now the foot of Trumbull, Hull ordered his men to retreat into the fort. British General Sir Isaac Brock ordered his troops to fire at the fort and several men were killed.

Many families came to the fort for protection, and it was impossible for cannon balls not to kill someone inside the fort as the population was dense in a small, enclosed area. Hull ordered his son, Captain A.F. Hull, to display a white flag. Many under Hull's command were indignant. General Lewis Cass broke his sword rather than giving it up to the enemy, setting an example for many others.

Citizens and soldiers accused Hull of cowardice. Hull defended his surrender by claiming he did so to prevent more bloodshed.

With England controlling Detroit again, many families left town for Ohio or New York. The British wanted some sort of continuity and left Judge Woodward in office.

Within days after the surrender, General Brock left Detroit and put Colonel Henry Proctor in command. Proctor hated and feared Americans, and he looked the other way as Indians capitalized on the situation. Indians often looted merchants and carted off livestock from farms.

Proctor's silence emboldened the Indians. The attacks became more savage and led to massacres of American soldiers down south. Those who weren't killed were brought back and mistreated in public to arouse the pity of Detroit's citizenry to pay a ransom. Even some British officers helped ransom American soldiers from the Indians.

While the Indians were pillaging and profiting, former Governor Hull stood trial in Washington for treason. Found guilty and sentenced to be shot, President James Madison pardoned him because he was almost 60 and had been a hero in the Revolutionary War.

Washington D.C. didn't forget about Detroit. Army troops underwent training in Ohio over the winter of 1812 and 1813 with the intention of liberating the town. In the meantime, Woodward was able to carry out some of his plans. He laid out subdivisions all over the area and called one of them Ypsilanti, in honor of his military idol, the Greek general in the Grecian revolt against the Turks.

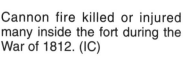

Cannon fire killed or injured many inside the fort during the War of 1812. (IC)

Lewis Cass (JB)

The British, afraid of a revolt by Detroiters, ordered all citizens to take an oath of allegiance to the King of England. Father Gabriel Richard refused, claiming he took an oath to uphold the constitution of the United States. Richard was arrested, sent across the river to Sandwich (now Windsor), and put in prison.

Freedom was near for Richard and Detroit as American troops won battles in Canada and reoccupied Detroit on September 29, 1813. Freedom reigned, but prosperity didn't as food was scarce and the planting of crops had been interrupted by war. Things got worse as a cholera-like epidemic swept through town, killing many soldiers. They were buried in common graves at the northeast corner of Cass and Michigan.

Shortages of food and livestock forced many citizens to exist on boiled hay. Washington granted Judge Woodward's appeal for relief and slowly things returned to normal. Fort Lernoult was renamed Fort Shelby, in honor of General Isaac Shelby, the governor of Kentucky and a war hero who helped save Detroit.

Lewis Cass, who was named governor of the Michigan territory October 29, 1813, would continue to hold that post for another 19 years. Cass worked hard for Michiganders and won the respect of the Indians too. Detroit's population was around 350 in 1813, and the entire Territory of Michigan had fewer than 5,000 residents. Indian attacks were no longer feared, but new settlers were bypassing Michigan and heading to Ohio, Indiana and Illinois. Easterners knew the way to Detroit was a long, hard ground journey across Canada or Ohio. The lakes were the only other alternative, but that was slow and expensive.

Cass countered Michigan's poor image with marketing. Tourists were invited to come see the area, and President Monroe was persuaded to visit Detroit in 1817. Cass made sure the presidential visit was publicized in the East and did the same when other well-known visitors passed through. Slowly the image of Michigan began to change.

It was also a time of change in the religious and educational spheres. The First Evangelistic Society of Detroit was organized to hold Protestant church services, and the first issue of the four-page *Detroit Gazette* was published for fewer than a hundred subscribers.

Except for this small newspaper, there was little to read. There were few volumes in the Detroit City Library, as it was organized by citizens who sold subscriptions for the purchase of books. The library was housed in the new building on Bates between Larned and Congress. This marked the beginning of the University of Michigan. Reverend John Monteith was the president and Father Gabriel Richard the vice president. These two men also held all the professorships.

The following year steamboats carrying passengers from Buffalo arrived. Families came from New York to settle in an oak forest—later to become Oakland County—and named their area after familiar New York towns such as Rochester.

By 1820 Detroit's population of 1,422 included 6 percent free blacks. The first post roads were opened to Pontiac and Mt. Clemens, and two years later stagecoaches began running.

Judge Woodward was finally run out of town in 1824. For the past 19 years, Woodward had held court whenever he wanted, even in the wee hours of the morning when he would often eat and drink while listening to testimony. Woodward, reputedly a two-bottle-a-day man, occasionally fell out of the chair he used as a judge's bench, and he regularly slept under a pear tree on what would become the site of Old City Hall.

A big banquet and bonfire helped celebrate the departure of Woodward and the beginning of elected officials. John R. Williams campaigned to become Detroit's first mayor. There were two John Williams in the city, so to distinguish himself from the other, the mayoral aspirant wanted folks to refer to him as "John R." A military hero and in business with his uncle, Joseph Campau, John R. Williams became mayor and his first name and middle initial became one of Detroit's famous streets.

While Woodward was history, his plan lingered. It called for a state capitol to be built at Grand Circus Park, but it was still too far out in the country, so a small triangular piece of real estate fronting on State Street was selected. The capitol building was completed in 1828, and today the area is known as Capitol Park.

While the capitol was under construction in 1826, Wayne County was reduced to its present

John R. Williams (JB)

boundaries and Detroiters had a weekly paper called the *Michigan Herald Weekly*. Troops stationed at Detroit were removed and the Fort Shelby area was donated to the city by Congress. Demolition of the fort began, and the earth from the fort embankments was deposited along the riverfront, a project that would take another eight years. The wall around the city was removed in 1827 and the neighborhood north of Fort Street began to expand.

Although it was taking longer and longer to walk around the growing town, strollers now had sidewalks, thanks to a City Council ordinance. Sidewalks were usually built of wooden planks, as cement didn't come into use until around the end of the century.

Trees were being felled for new homes and sidewalks as new residents came to town via the Erie Canal. Opened in late 1825, the canal connected the eastern seaboard with the Great Lakes. Easterners connecting to Buffalo came to Detroit in five and a half days. Before the canal it took two months longer to make it to Detroit.

More residents meant more mail and more work for postmaster James Abbott. His wife also helped. Mrs. Abbott was the aunt of the famous artist James Abbott McNeil Whistler. The post office at this time was located at Woodward and Woodbridge, now the site of the Windsor tunnel. William Woodbridge was the first delegate from the Michigan Territory to Congress in 1819 and in the same year he bought the acreage that would one day include Tiger Stadium. In the 1820s Woodbridge supervised the building of the Chicago Road, following the route of the old Sauk Trail, which would later become Michigan Avenue.

The Macombs, a wealthy Detroit family, owned most of Macomb County, along with Grosse Ile and Belle Isle. Alexander Macomb, a talented artist, chose a military career. A war hero in 1812, he became Commander of Detroit and later was appointed Commanding General of the Army of the United States.

Right: The bronze and granite statue of General Alexander Macomb is located on Washington Boulevard at Michigan Avenue. (JF)

Below: Detroit in 1826 from a drawing by General Alexander Macomb. (BHC)

1830-1874

The fur trade wasn't much of an economic factor for Detroit by 1830, as the town boasted of 232 diverse businesses among its 2,222 residents. The population was reduced by one when Stephen Simmons was hanged for killing his wife. The hanging—the last in Michigan—took place on what is now the site of the Downtown Library on Gratiot.

John R. Williams, who was still mayor, gave birth to the weekly *Democratic Free Press and Michigan Intelligencer*—the forerunner of the *Detroit Free Press*—the following year. Lewis Cass moved up the political ladder as he accepted the position of Secretary of War in President Andrew Jackson's cabinet. George B. Porter succeeded Cass as governor of the Michigan Territory. Porter didn't have good work habits, however, and Stevens T. Mason, the competent 19-year-old territorial secretary, frequently served as acting governor.

1832 was a disastrous year. As a steamer carrying 300 soldiers neared Detroit, an illness felled several. The vessel docked and health officials were called to examine the men. They confirmed the illness as cholera and ordered the ship to depart. The cholera spread quickly among the men as the ship sailed. When it docked again in Port Huron, many men jumped ship and tried to make it back to

Detroit in the 1830s. (BHC)

Stevens T. Mason (JB)

Fr. Gabriel Richard was the last victim of the cholera epidemic in 1832. (JB)

Looking northeast from Griswold and Jefferson in 1837 when Michigan became the 26th state. The First Methodist Episcopal Church (center) and the First Presbyterian church were on the east side of Woodward between Congress and Larned. Looming in the distance were the twin spires of Ste. Anne's. (BHC)

Detroit. Most died along the way, but the ones who made it brought the dreaded disease.

Many Detroiters, fearing for their lives, fled and tried to enter nearby towns. The news traveled faster than they did, though, and roads were barricaded and armed guards posted. Horses were shot as their riders tried to gain entry. Others got the message and came back to Detroit, where they found Father Gabriel Richard aiding the sick and dying. Cholera claimed Father Richard 69 days after the first vic-tim. All told, 96 died from the disease

Cholera struck again two years later and claimed over 600 victims, including Governor Porter. Despite the hardships, Detroit gained new residents. In 1836, Detroit's population was 6,927. With almost 200 free blacks in Wayne County, the Second Baptist Church, the first black church in Michigan Territory, was founded. Three years earlier, the town's first Lutheran church was established.

Also in 1836, William Woodbridge, who would

Residence of Lewis Cass, built around 1840, at the northwest corner of Fort and Cass. (BHC)

If Cass could look out his front window today, this is what he'd see. (IC)

go on to become governor and a United States Senator, named a dirt road that ran through his property Trumbull, after his father-in-law, poet John Trumbull. Trumbull, the eastern boundary of the Woodbridge farm, became the western city limit of Detroit.

Lewis Cass, the richest man in the area at the time, added to his wealth. Cass had a farm of more than 500 acres that extended from the Detroit River for three miles; its width today would be from Cass Avenue to Third Street. Cass sold it for more than half a million dollars but reserved two parcels of land, which he donated to the city. One parcel became the site of Cass High School, and the other was dedicated for public use as Cass Park, across from the Masonic Temple.

It was a good time for business, and some of Detroit's leading businessmen at this time were Edmund Brush, Shubael Conant, Elon Farnsworth, Eurotas P. Hastings, and Charles Trowbridge. It was a peaceful time as Henry Rowe Schoolcraft was in charge of Indian affairs for Michigan and arranged peace treaties between the tribes and Michiganders.

The area was booming. The first underground sewer was built and on one single day in May of 1836, more than 2,400 settlers poured into town. The arrival of from seven to 10 steamboats a day wasn't uncommon. The following year on May 28, 31 boats of some type arrived and a city directory was published.

Michigan was formally admitted to the Union as the 26th state on January 26, 1837. Polish settlers first began to come to town, and Irish immigrants were settling south of Michigan Avenue. Since many came from County Cork, the area they were moving into became known as Corktown.

While whites had freedom of movement, blacks were restricted. Many whites tried to remedy the situation and formed the Detroit Anti Slavery Society. Detroit became a station on the Underground Railroad, and escaped slaves were housed in the Finney Barn on the northeast corner of State and Griswold until they could safely be escorted to freedom in Canada.

In 1838 Detroit's first public school opened. Class was held in a little wooden two-story building built on piles on the shore of the river near Shelby—about where Convention Arena is today. The lower part was used as a grocery store, and the upper floor was the school. Another little wooden building at Michigan and Griswold housed the Michigan Central Railroad. Two trains daily made the round trip to Ypsilanti.

Trains were going farther and more residents came to town. Detroit's population reached 9,124 in 1840, and the city started to become a leading tobacco manufacturing center. The Mayor, Dr. Zina Pitcher, pushed for a city tax to provide free education to children between the ages of four and 18. Pitcher became president of the board of education and became known through the generations as the father of Detroit's public school system.

During the 1840s the European revolutions brought many foreigners to America. Cities wanted the new immigrants to help spur growth. In fact, many states sent agents to New York to expound on the merits of their area in order to lure new residents. Michigan sent an agent to New York in 1845 to spread the word that the state was linked to the East by a transportation network of water and rail lines. At this time it took two weeks by train to reach Chicago from New York. It took nine days for a letter from New York to reach Detroit.

Work continued from the previous year on Grand Circus Park as it was drained, filled, and raised. Belle Isle became more attractive simply by shedding its former name, Hog Island.

Street corner talk in 1847 centered around the shift of the state capital from Detroit to Lansing. The old capitol building would be used as a school. Telegraph service began between Detroit and Ypsilanti and would reach New York and Chicago the following year. Communication and transportation were expanding and a new Michigan Central Depot was being built at Michigan and Third Streets.

Main streets such as Woodward, Michigan, Grand River, and Gratiot were turned over to private companies for maintenance and repair in 1848. In return, entrepreneurs collected tolls to cover the cost of installing planks on the roads. Tollgates were usually placed 10 miles apart on each plank road. One of the busiest was on Woodward at Adams. A few years later, some planks were replaced by filling and grading the roads with gravel. Some toll roads remained for almost half a century.

The popular Uncle Ben's Steamboat Hotel was the establishment of the rich and famous and the scene of many big banquets and balls. "Uncle Ben" Woodworth was one of Detroit's leading celebrities. He had many titles including hangman, though the last time he had practiced that occupation was 18 years earlier.

The worst fire in almost half a century since the one that devastated Detroit in 1805 took place on a May Day in 1848. The whole lower area of the city, bounded by the river, Jefferson, Bates, and Brush was destroyed. The Steamboat Hotel was reduced to ashes.

Even a major fire couldn't stop Detroit's growth, though. Travelers kept coming and so did new residents.

One new resident was Lt. Ulysses S. Grant. His title was Commanding Officer of the Detroit Barracks. Many Detroiters, however, called Grant other things—such as a drunk. During his three-year stay in town, Grant built himself a bad reputation. He was notorious for driving his horse too fast through the streets, and on a cold January night, Grant slipped on the icy sidewalk outside of Zachariah Chandler's grocery store. Grant sent Chandler the doctor's bill for treatment of his injured ankle.

Chandler, a wealthy dry goods merchant, refused to pay and Grant sued. Chandler demanded a jury trial and conducted his own case, but admitted that he didn't clear his sidewalk.

"Soldiers are but idle loafers living off the tax paying community," Chandler addressed the court. "And, Lieutenant Grant," continued Chandler, "if you soldiers would only stay sober, perhaps you wouldn't fall on people's sidewalks."

Grant won the case but the jury only awarded him five cents. A few months later, the War Department closed the Detroit Barracks and Grant was shipped out of town.

While Grant left, others kept coming. The 1850 census showed 21,019 people living in Detroit. Mrs. Sarah Cozens thought there might be enough Jewish families to start a synagogue and offered her home on Congress near St. Antoine for services.

Mrs. Cozens and her husband Isaac found 51 Jews in town over the age of 18. The interested ones showed up and formed the Beth El Society. Through the years the congregation grew to be called Temple Beth El, and after several moves is now on Telegraph Road south of 15 Mile Road.

Zachariah Chandler (JB)

Detroit was growing fast from a town into a city. The beginning of the second half of the 19th century saw a Detroit with about 90 streets. Most residents lived near the river, but a few houses were scattered as far north as Grand Circus Park, with farms beyond. A curfew bell rang four times every 12 hours—at six o'clock in the morning, noon, six and nine at night—to give the time.

It was a prosperous time for Detroit and Detroiters. The rich got richer and the average Detroit worker got by on less than a dollar per day. Zachariah Chandler's fortunes went up and former Detroiter Ulysses S. Grant's went down.

Chandler's political career also grew as he became mayor in 1851, the year Grant left. Grant ended up in St. Louis after his army days. His father-in-law gave him a small farm and three slaves to do the work, but Grant was unsuccessful and also failed at real estate. He then tried a change of scenery and moved to Galena, Illinois, where he entered the hide tanning business with his brother.

After Grant's departure, Detroit had rail lines reaching Chicago, New York, Toledo, and Port Huron. Detroit also gained a telegraph cable laid across the Detroit River and ferries to Windsor; a railway car manufacturing company; a couple of chewing tobacco manufacturing businesses; a varnish factory; a new concert hall east of Cadillac Square; a leading hotel on Woodward called the Russell House; a high school in a new building on Broadway; the first superintendent of schools; an impressive second Presbyterian church building; a new physician by the name of Dr. Herman Kiefer; a new city charter providing a salary for the mayor for the first time; and to report it all, a new daily newspaper called, the Daily Free Democrat.

There were losses, too. Another cholera epidemic swept through town in 1854, claiming among its victims the only Jewish congregation's first rabbi. Also that year, John R. Williams, Detroit's first mayor 30 years earlier, died at the age of 72.

It was an age in which more people in Detroit spoke out against slavery. Prominent citizens, including Zachariah Chandler, founded a new political party to fight slavery called the Republican Party and three years later in 1857, Chandler was elected U.S. Senator from Michigan.

On March 12, 1859, John Brown, a white man, came to Detroit with 14 slaves to smuggle across the river to Canada to freedom. Brown, the fiery anti-

Left: Half an acre in Elmwood Cemetery's southeast corner was bought by Beth El as a separate cemetery. (IC)

Right: The cholera epidemic of 1854 claimed Detroit's first rabbi. (IC)

Right: William Webb's house on the north side of Congress near St. Antoine where John Brown and Frederick Douglass exchanged views with prominent members of Detroit's free negro community. (BHC)

Below: The First Michigan Volunteer Infantry had 780 men, as Detroiters gathered in Campus Martius to say farewell on May 13, 1861. About 6,000 Detroiters served in the Civil War. (BHC)

slavery leader, came to William Webb's house on Congress near St. Antoine with Frederick Douglass, a former slave and well-known orator and writer. Douglass sought freedom for slaves through political means and orderly democratic processes. Listening to opposing views on how slavery should be abolished were many prominent members of Detroit's Negro community.

Detroit had over 47,000 residents when President Lincoln proclaimed a state of war on April 17, 1861, and called for volunteers. Michigan answered and more than 90,000 men from the state served in the Civil War, 6,000 of whom were from Detroit. The war called on Michigan's Jewish families as 210 Jewish soldiers—more than one per family—served.

While many fathers were away, Detroit's school-children were divided into grades in 1862 and taught the three Rs—reading, writing and arithmetic. Other subjects were introduced but soon discarded as leading citizens thought children would become confused and not remember the three Rs.

Detroit's only high school, five years old in 1863, was moved to the second floor of the former capitol building at State and Griswold.

Children and adults could take the new horse-drawn cars which ran on rails laid on a mud foundation. As the new downtown travel era dawned, Henry Ford was born in Dearborn and Detroit's wealthiest man, Joseph Campau, died.

While the Civil War seemed far away, civil behavior in Detroit was in danger. Violence and theft were common as the main commercial streets and the waterfront were deserted at night. Burglaries and muggings were happening at an alarming rate. Merchants were worried and suspicious as they locked their establishments at night and didn't feel any safer when they returned home, as the better neighborhoods were targeted by thieves.

Negroes were targeted on the morning of March 6, 1863, when a mob of hoodlums rampaged along Brush and Beaubien south of Gratiot. Many were beaten and their homes looted and torched, while others escaped the mayhem and sought refuge in Canada. The riot was touched off when an angry

mob tried to lynch a black man accused of raping two nine-year-old girls—one of whom was white. Authorities held the mob in check while getting the prisoner to safety. The angry mob then turned their attention to the nearby neighborhood. When the riot ended, 35 structures had been destroyed by 20 fires. The prisoner—named William Faulkner—was later proven innocent when the girls admitted they fabricated the charges.

Detroit's population charged ahead and passed 53,400 in 1864. The Young Mens Christian Association was established and some newcomers played, prayed, and stayed at the YMCA.

Harper Hospital opened—the result of gifts from Nancy Martin and Walter Harper—as a military hospital to care for the Civil War wounded. Nancy Martin, a sharp-tongued woman not known for her attractiveness, operated a chicken and vegetable stall in Cadillac Square's Public Market. Miss Martin invested her savings in a five-acre farm on property that today is the Medical Center. Walter Harper, who became wealthy with extensive real estate holdings, boarded obscurely on the Martin farm.

Farms were short of help during the war as able-bodied men were in demand. The First Michigan Colored Infantry, numbering 1,673 black troops, was mustered, increasing the demand for laborers.

Mail was extremely important to families waiting to hear from men serving in the war. In October 1864, free mail delivery by carriers began in Detroit. Iron letter boxes on lamp posts of grocery and drug stores were introduced to Detroiters for outgoing mail.

Meanwhile, back at the warfront, former Detroiter Ulysses S. Grant was gaining a reputation for winning many battles, even though his forces suffered heavy casualties. President Lincoln wanted to reward Grant with the rank of General but was advised Grant had a drinking problem and that it might not be a good idea to promote such a man. After several reminders, Lincoln rose and addressed his advisers:

"Gentlemen," Lincoln said as he stood and looked at those present, "find out what Grant drinks and send all the generals a case."

Grant's old Detroit nemesis, Zachariah Chandler, was the big man of the Congressional Committee on the Conduct of the War. Grant and Chandler buried the hatchet and talked about the good old days in Detroit while toasting the future.

In April 1865, Detroiters celebrated the news of the fall of Richmond and the surrender of the confederacy. An Arch of Triumph was placed at Woodward and Jefferson to welcome back the hometown troops to the growing city of 65,000.

The celebration was short-lived as men and women sobbed openly in the streets over the news of the assassination of President Lincoln. The front page of the *Detroit Free Press* on Saturday, April 15, 1865 told it in black borders:

> *"The President is Assassinated."*
> *"He is shot at the Theatre."*
> *"Escape of the Assassin."*

Shock and disbelief faded and life went on. Detroit was jolted again the following year when Lewis Cass died at the age of 84. Cass, who was Secretary of State when the Civil War broke out, was buried in Elmwood Cemetery after a long funeral procession witnessed by thousands of mourners.

After his discharge from the Union Army, James Vernor opened his own drugstore at the southwest corner of Woodward and Clifford and called it "The Farthest North Drug Store." It was pretty far north in those days. When he had time, Vernor toyed with a new drink, sold his first ginger ale at the store, and the rest is history.

James Robinson, a black man, saw a lot of history. He fought in the American Revolution and in the War of 1812. Robinson, who was Detroit's oldest man when he died in 1868 at age 115, was buried in Elmwood Cemetery.

Many new homes went up in 1869, including Governor John J. Bagley's mansion at Park and Washington. It would stand until early the next century when the site would house the new Statler Hotel.

The Old Biddle House was the leading hotel at

Above: Six Michigan governors, eleven U.S. Senators, thirty Detroit mayors, and numerous prominent individuals are among the 55,000 or so buried on the grounds of Elmwood Cemetery.(IC)

Right: Hills and valleys make up much of the terrain at Elmwood. This tree dates back to the early days of Detroit. (IC)

that time. Across the street from the Old Union Depot Building on East Jefferson, it was handy for travelers. James Macauley, 22, moved to town from Rochester, New York, and set up shop in the depot to sell stationery, magazines and books. It marked the birth of Macauley's Office Products.

The Detroit Opera House facing Campus Martius opened and Negro children were first admitted to Detroit's public schools. Now that the Civil War was over, the states may have been reunited on maps, but not in the minds of many, as the Ku Klux Klan was organized and the movement gained momentum in the South.

Ulysses S. Grant, who failed at occupations other than soldiering, became President of the United States in 1869 and named Zachariah Chandler to his cabinet as Secretary of the Interior.

William Davis, who owned a small Detroit fish market near Third and Howard, invented a refrigerator car to ship fresh meat, fish, and fruit. George Hammond, who had a prosperous meat packing business nearby, tried shipping a carload to Boston and was so happy with the result that he bought the patent from Davis. Soon the George Hammond Company had a fleet of refrigerator cars and was king of shipping food by rail.

At the same time Parke, Davis & Company was becoming one of the kings in the pharmaceutical

Above: A watchman, stationed in the tower of City Hall to look for fires, checks the Campus Martius area. (BHC)

Left: Detroit's first paid fire department was established in 1867. (BHC)

field. The company began as Duffield, Parke & Company after the Civil War in a small store on lower Woodward. George Davis joined the growing business in 1867 and became a partner after Dr. Samuel Duffield, a chemist and physician, went back to private practice two years later. Davis and Hervey Parke became the chief operating officers and steered the company to larger quarters and profits.

Detroit grew larger by 1870 with a population of 79,577, doubling in less than 15 years. There were about 16,000 voters in the city and blacks finally had the right to vote as Michigan's citizens voted to eliminate the word "white" from the U.S. constitution.

With over $1 million in resources in 1871, the Detroit Savings Fund Institute, founded 22 years earlier, changed its name to Detroit Savings Bank. At the time, the forerunner of Comerica Bank was located where the Guardian Building stands today. Across the street was George Pattison's busy book store. Up the street, the magnificent, newly opened City Hall could be seen, and around the corner at Lafayette and running west to Trumbull, the streets boasted the first cedar paving blocks, roughly the shape of a brick.

On Woodward between Congress and Cadillac Square, Christopher Mabley opened a clothing store and became the city's first merchant to market his establishment by buying full page newspaper ads. George Pullman became well-known when he purchased the Detroit Car and Manufacturing Company and Detroit became the center of manufacturing Pullman cars for trains.

The police department introduced patrol wagons and a state law required children between the ages of eight and 14 to attend school for at least 12 weeks each year.

The following year, Mayor Hugh Moffatt, who supervised the construction of the Moffatt Building on the southwest corner of Fort and Griswold, opened the four-story structure containing Detroit's

The Soldiers and Sailors' Monument was unveiled April 9, 1872. (IC)

first elevator. Detroiters of privilege went to the top of the building to view the ceremonies dedicating the Soldiers and Sailors' Monument on Woodward at Campus Martius. Throngs of Civil War veterans and families beamed proudly at the monument honoring the sacrifices of Michiganders during the war.

James Scripps, who chronicled many of the events in Detroit in his role as editor and manager of the Detroit Advertiser, decided to publish the Evening News, predecessor of the Detroit News. The first issue was published on August 23, 1873, and it sold for two cents while others charged five cents.

All the papers covered the news regarding the growth of Parke Davis & Company and its new location on the river near the foot of Joseph Campau.

1875-1889

On the west side of Woodward north of Michigan Avenue, Fred Sanders opened his ice cream and candy store in 1875. Sanders is credited with inventing the ice cream soda, hitting upon the idea one sweltering day when all of his cream soured.

City officials took a 20-year lease on most of Woodbridge Grove for a much-needed wood and hay market and dog pound. The area around Michigan and Trumbull streets was cleared of trees and shrubbery and paved with cobblestones. Farmers now had a large market from which to sell their lumber and hay on the western edge of the city.

Sanders made its debut on Woodward in 1875. (MV)

The city experimented with different kinds of paving and tried asphalt for the first time in 1877 on Jefferson between Woodward and Brush. A few blocks north, the impressive new Detroit Public Library opened at Gratiot and Farmer streets. The interior featured 10 large cast iron columns through three levels.

For those preferring viewing to reading, Detroit had several theaters. Matinees were usually on Tuesday and Friday afternoons and admission ranged from 15 to 50 cents.

Detroiters were talking about—and some were talking on—the first telephone in the city, only one year after its invention by Alexander Graham Bell.

Thirty-four years before it would be renamed University of Detroit in 1911, Detroit College was founded on East Jefferson, adjoining Saints Peter and Paul Roman Catholic Church. Further east on Jefferson, Detroit had several stove producing plants, making the city the stove-making capital of the world.

Joseph Lowthian Hudson moved to Detroit in 1877 to manage Mabley's clothing department. Mabley's continued to expand on Woodward and featured all kinds of merchandise for the family. Mabley soon had stores on both sides of Woodward to house his expanding business consisting mainly of clothing, furniture, and shoes.

A year after Detroit's first telephone line linked Stearns' Drugstore at Woodward and Jefferson to his laboratory at Woodbridge and Sixth, the city's first telephone directory in 1878 listed 124 customers. Detroiters were dazzled again when the first phonograph in the area was exhibited.

In 1879 Detroit's telephone customers were the country's first to be assigned phone numbers to facilitate handling calls. Detroiters were getting used to new inventions and a busier city, and many weren't happy that Belle Isle was becoming a city-owned park. The island was inaccessible except by boat and was excellent for hunting and fishing, but the city had visions of families picnicking and playing.

With 1880 less than eight weeks away, the mood in town turned sour as Senator Zachariah Chandler died while in Chicago. His body was brought back by a committee of leading citizens and thousands of Detroiters viewed and joined the funeral cortege to Elmwood Cemetery.

Detroit's booming economy was fueled by its tobacco, stove, and pharmaceutical industries, and the business section of downtown was pushing north of Campus Martius in 1880 as the city's population topped 116,000.

Saints Peter and Paul Roman Catholic Church at Jefferson and St. Antoine was built in 1848 and is the oldest edifice of worship in Detroit. The adjoining college was founded in 1877.

The Detroit Stove Works boasted it was the largest stove factory in the world and made 30,000 stoves per year. Thirteen hundred workers produced 700 models of stoves at the company's 10-acre site near Belle Isle.

A reminder of the past, Joseph Campau's old log house on the south side of Jefferson between Griswold and Shelby was demolished. The house, which outlived its owner, had been painted yellow, a colorful relic of Detroit's village days.

More progress came in the form of an electric light which was publicly exhibited in front of the Detroit Opera House in Campus Martius. Six months later, several stores along Woodward had electrical current powered from a small generator in the basement of the *Detroit Free Press* Building.

A new central market was opened in Cadillac Square with the front entrance facing the eastern side of the Soldiers and Sailors' Monument. Meat stalls occupied the first floor, while the upper two floors housed local government agencies. The older vegetable market remained in the eastern end of Cadillac Square.

International communications were established via a phone line linking Detroit and Windsor. More women were being hired as phone operators, replacing previously hired males.

Eleven-year-old Albert Kahn came to town from Germany with his family, and 17-year-old Henry Ford left his family in Dearborn and found a job at a Detroit machine shop for $2.50 a week.

While Detroit's black population numbered

Looking across the Detroit Opera House and Campus Martius to the west side of Woodward in 1888. (from the Manning Brothers Historic Photo Collection)

2,921—almost 2.5 percent of the city's population—most were forced to accept menial employment because of discrimination. Some became businessmen within their own community by operating stores, hotels, saloons, and restaurants.

One of the most famous blacks living in Detroit was an inventor. Elijah McCoy came to Michigan after the Civil War. A mechanical engineer trained in Scotland, discrimination forced him to become a railroad fireman where he patented an automatic lubricating cup that eliminated the need for frequent stops for oiling. McCoy's company manufactured lubricators for locomotives and steamships around the world. The expression, "the real McCoy," originated in Detroit and referred to McCoy's quality merchandise.

Joseph L. Hudson, manager of clothing merchandise for Mabley's, opened his own clothing store on the ground floor of the Detroit Opera House in Campus Martius. Robert B. Tannahill, also an employee of Mabley's, went to work for J.L. Hudson and stayed with the company for another 42 years before retiring in 1923 as vice president.

Pro baseball began in 1881 as Detroit became a member of the National League. Cincinnati, a charter member of the league, which was organized in 1876, dropped out in 1880 and Detroit filled the vacancy.

There were plenty of indoor forms of entertainment to watch, as many performers made regular stops in Detroit on the show business circuit. Actress Sarah Bernhardt appeared at Whitney's Grand Opera House on the corner of Shelby and Fort.

While the city was using the Michigan and Trumbull area around the Woodbridge Farm for a hay market, Dudley Woodbridge leased the remain-

The Detroit Opera House in Campus Martius had space for rent when Hudson's vacated and moved around the corner to the west side of Woodward. (BHC)

Ste.-Anne de Detroit is the oldest parish in the city. It was founded July 26, 1701, two days after Cadillac landed and founded Detroit. This structure was built in 1886 and is located near the Ambassador Bridge on Lafayette and St. Anne. (courtesy Ste. Anne Roman Catholic Church)

der to a lumber company in 1882. Woodbridge also donated land on the south side of Michigan Avenue for use as a zoo. The animals had been abandoned by circuses suffering financial hardships.

James McGinnis was born on the site of what is now Cobo Hall and changed his last name to Bailey when he bought the Cooper and Bailey Touring Worldwide Circus. He teamed up with Phineas T. Barnum in 1881 and the circus became known as the Barnum and Bailey Circus.

Civil War hero Russell A. Alger, who had various local contacts through his lumber business and interests in banking, manufacturing and railroads, was elected governor of Michigan in 1884.

1880 photo of houses on Edmund Street in the Brush Park district, located a few blocks north of where Comerica Park stands today. (MV)

The same scene today. (MV)

The city contracted for lighting the streets by electricity, and 72 iron skeleton towers from 104 to 150 feet high were constructed. During business hours, the area on Woodward between Campus Martius and Grand River was so crowded that policemen were needed at crosswalks to escort ladies and children across the street.

There was plenty of news to report, and the *Evening News* published its first Sunday edition in November. Detroit had over 30 brewers at this time, and one family—the Strohs—would even gain more fame.

Capitalizing on his fame, Sitting Bull had star billing as Buffalo Bill Cody and his Wild West Company appeared in Detroit in June 1885.

The following year, streetcars of the Highland Park Railway began running on Woodward, and deer, which were running free on Belle Isle, were zoned into a deer park, marking the beginning of the Belle Isle Zoo.

George Hammond, who grew wealthy by shipping fresh meat in refrigerated rail cars, died. At the time of his death, his company operated a thousand cars. His widow continued with plans to build Detroit's tallest building on the corner of west Fort and Griswold.

In 1887 J.L. Hudson moved his growing business from the ground floor of the Detroit Opera House to the west side of Woodward between Michigan Avenue and State Street.

There was a parade through the streets to Woodward as the Detroits—the city's pro baseball club— won the National League championship. The team played at Recreation Park on Brady between John R. and Brush—not too far north from where home plate at Comerica Park lies today. There was no such thing as a World Series, as the American League wouldn't be born until the turn of the century.

Tobacco tycoon Daniel Scotten owned the corner of Washington Boulevard and Michigan Avenue. The site had several hotels since 1836, and Scotten decided the time was ripe in 1888 for a larger one. He named the new 200-room hotel the Cadillac, after the city's founder.

The Cadillac Hotel on the corner of Washington Boulevard and Michigan Avenue opened in 1888.

The city's sewer system periodically flooded basements of stores along a section of Woodward, and the local alderman from the second ward, Seymour Finney, opposed the building of a new one. James Vernor decided to run against him on this issue and won, thus becoming as well known for his politics as for his ginger ale.

Hazen Pingree, who owned a shoe business, was elected mayor and began a regime of reforming city services, concentrating on the utilities and transportation system.

Belle Isle had its first bridge in 1889. Prior to the opening of the bridge, riding the Belle Isle ferry was a favorite pastime. For 10 cents one could ride back and forth all day, which some people did on hot days.

Ellen Hammond, widow of George Hammond, proudly opened the 10-story Hammond Building. It was one of the largest masonry structures in the country at the time. To celebrate the opening of Detroit's tallest building, a high-wire performer successfully completed a cable walk stretched high above Fort Street from the Hammond Building to the City Hall tower.

The Hammond Building, on the corner of West Fort and Griswold, was opened in 1889.

THE 1890s

Detroit in 1890 had 205,876 residents, a population gain of 160,257 in only thirty years. Detroit teachers began the 1890s earning $30 a month at entry level and a maximum of $70 after nine years. Streetcar drivers received a raise to $1.50 a day and barbers raised the price of a shave to 15 cents. Albert Kahn earned a $500 scholarship to study architecture abroad.

Joseph L. Hudson was satisfied with his architect's design as he opened an eight-story de-

Woodward meets the Detroit River in 1890. (MV)

partment store at Gratiot and Farmer in 1891. Times were good and the store with four elevators on each floor was an immediate success.

Detroit's first black policeman, Joseph Stowers, was fired after only two months on the job. White officers were behind anonymous letters charging Stowers with all sorts of improper acts, charges that were false.

There were changes in the streets as asphalt came into use. Four streets—Jefferson, Cass, Lafayette and Second—had it by 1892.

The YMCA established the Detroit College of Law in 1892. The Detroit Institute of Technology had been born a year earlier at the Y.

Rival gas light companies merged in 1893, giving birth to the Michigan Consolidated Gas Company, making electricity for home lighting available. Electric streetcars operated on Woodward. Ernst Kern opened his store on Monroe and Randolph that year.

Detroit had about 4,000 phones by the mid-1890s, and long distance service was established to Chicago and New York. Mrs. Marie Owen made news when she was appointed the first policewoman in the United States.

Former U.S. Senator Thomas Palmer donated his estate to the city for use as a park. Most people, however, would find Palmer Park just too far up Woodward to travel to.

Henry Ford was now earning $75 monthly working at Detroit Edison's powerhouse and his first child Edsel was born.

The old Capitol Building, which was used as a school, burned, and the city developed the damaged area into Capitol Park. Popular Hazen Pingree, who always dressed properly and wore a frock coat on top of the latest in male fashion, was elected mayor for a third term.

Before Pingree could be sworn in, however, the national economic crisis worsened. More railroads went broke and more than 500 banks around the country failed, idling a quarter of all heavy industry. The depression of 1894 hit Detroit hard and soon funds for many of the city's 25,000 jobless had run out.

Mayor Pingree urged real estate speculators holding vacant land to use their properties for the growing of vegetables and potatoes. Pingree also appealed for funds to purchase gardening tools. He set an example by selling his favorite horse and using the funds to buy seeds and tools. Soon Pingree's ideas and implementations were picked up by newspapers in other cities.

New York papers coined Detroit's Mayor, "Potato Patch Pingree." More publicity meant more donations, and Detroit's real estate barons responded by lending their acreage. Mayor Pingree was often seen digging and planting, endearing him further to Detroit's populace. Besides being fed, the poor and unemployed were kept busy digging, planting, harvesting, and distributing.

Mayor Pingree was also seen on the city's streetcars often, acting as the conductor and driver. Un-

Hazen Pingree was the mayor of Detroit and the governor of Michigan at the same time. (IC)

der his administration, he built more than 50 miles of new track, lowered fares, and removed toll gates from the principal streets. There were four toll gates on Woodward, which annoyed streetcar passengers. One was at Adams, another near the present area of Grand Boulevard, one north of Seven Mile, and another south of Birmingham.

Newspapers around the country carried the sad report of Charlie Bennett's tragic accident. Bennett, the catcher on Detroit's championship baseball team of 1887, was on an off-season hunting trip to Kansas in 1894 when he tried to board a moving train but lost his balance and fell beneath the cars.

Bennett's left foot was severed and his right leg was later amputated below the knee. Detroiters sent Bennett cards and letters while he was undergoing treatment, inspiring the former baseball hero to move back to Detroit to operate a cigar store and benefit from his fame.

Bennett left Detroit as the city's baseball fortunes

Charlie Bennett, catcher on Detroit's first championship baseball club, had a ballpark named after him.

dwindled. After the club finished fifth in 1888, the franchise was transferred to Cleveland and later folded. Except for a 29-game stint in the Northwestern League, Detroit was without professional baseball for four years until joining the new Federal League in 1894. During this period, Bennett continued his major league career in Boston.

Detroit's Western League ball club played in tiny Boulevard Park at Lafayette and Helen, not far from the Belle Isle bridge. The 1895 season opened to enthusiastic cheering as Mayor Pingree threw out the ceremonial first pitch. While Pingree was popular, the cheers were mostly reserved for Bennett as he caught Pingree's toss while navigating on artificial limbs.

After the 1895 season, the owner of the Tigers, as the ball club was starting to be called, sought a location for a bigger ballpark and decided on the corner of Michigan and Trumbull. Fans and newsmen suggested the new park should be named after Charlie Bennett and were calling it Bennett Park even before construction was completed. Tigers owner George Vanderbeck wanted to please his customers and agreed to call his new ballyard after the former catcher.

Bennett Park opened on Tuesday, April 28, 1896, and Wayne County Treasurer Alex McLeod threw the ceremonial first pitch to Bennett. While different politicians would throw out the ceremonial first pitch in the coming years, Bennett would be on the other end for decades to come.

Horse-drawn passenger cars that had operated for decades ceased, and electric streetcars came into use. Detroiters were getting used to reading about and seeing new forms of transportation.

On March 6, 1896, Charles Brady King, a 27-year-old college-trained engineer, became the first person in Michigan to publicly drive a gasoline-powered horseless carriage. Despite two years of private testing on Belle Isle, King's handmade vehicle broke down on its test drive on Detroit's streets.

Almost three months after King's test drive, Henry Ford wheeled his own horseless vehicle from the yard of his home on Bagley (now the site of the

Michigan Theater parking structure and office building). Ford's horseless carriage was called the "quadricycle" because it ran on four bicycle tires. It had a four-horsepower, two-cylinder engine, and the whole contraption weighed 500 pounds.

Ford's first test drive went south from his home on Bagley, east to Grand River to Washington Boulevard, and south on the boulevard before the machine stopped because one of the ignitors failed. Ford immediately repaired it and drove back to his Bagley residence. Over the following months, Ford continued his test drives while his assistant bicycled ahead and stopped at saloons and stores to tell people to come out and hold their horses.

Ever since the Hammond Building was com-

pleted, businessman C.R. Mabley, who had his establishment on Woodward, dreamed of housing his department store in a structure that would be the tallest in Detroit. Mabley spent $700,000—a fantastic sum at the time—for frontage on Woodward and Michigan, where the First Federal Bank Building is today. Mabley proudly had a large "M" placed on the cornerstone and one on each of the hundreds of brass knobs on the office doors. Mabley was looking forward to the day when the Mabley Building would top the Hammond Building, but he died before the project was completed.

New owners took over but were saddled with "M's" everywhere. Since the building was the tallest and most majestic in the city, they named it the Ma-

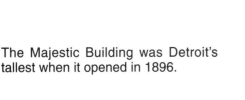

The Majestic Building was Detroit's tallest when it opened in 1896.

MAJESTIC BUILDING, DETROIT.

jestic Building. Sightseers who previously went to the top of the Hammond Building now went to the 14th story of the Majestic Building and for 10 cents could climb a flight of stairs to the observatory on the roof.

Hazen Pingree enjoyed puttering around his mansion on Woodward and Farnsworth, near where the art museum is today. Feeling a bit restless and somewhat smug about being elected Mayor of Detroit four times, Pingree ran for governor and won in 1896 while still mayoring. Pingree wanted to remain in both positions but the Supreme Court decided that the governor would have to choose which political office he wanted to work in. Pingree chose to govern the state but wanted the capitol moved back to Detroit where there were more choices and people.

While Pingree was the state's leading white politician, Robert Pelham probably was the leading black one. In 1896 Pelham was active in the Republican National Convention and held local and national government positions.

Also well-known was William Ferguson, the first black child admitted to Detroit's public schools in 1871. He became Michigan's first black legislator 22 years later and was often in the news on civil rights issues.

Central High School opened as an integrated school in an imposing new building on Cass and Warren. Decades later the structure would be known as "Old Main" in the Wayne State University complex.

Ernst Kern was only 22 years old but was a veteran of the family department store business and guided the growing establishment to a new location at Woodward and Gratiot, north of Campus Martius.

Campus Martius' centerpiece, the Detroit Opera House, was destroyed by fire a short time before Kerns moved in, in October 1897. Detroit's new Mayor William Maybury and other officials surveyed the scene and work to rebuild the city's famed entertainment center began almost immediately.

Sales were heating up for Detroit's several stove companies in 1898 as over 3,000 workers produced

The Majestic Building boasted that its Majestic Servself had a serving capacity of over 1,000 persons an hour.

165,000 stoves. The average wage of Michigan laborers at the time was $1.62 per day, and a pound of bread went for five cents.

For amusement, people checked out the newly rebuilt Detroit Opera House and crowds flocked to see the new jumpy moving pictures. The most popular of the two silent shorts was *The Empire State Express*. Audiences delighted in the moving train that seemed to be heading straight for them.

Wonderland, which housed many types of entertainment from animals to orchestras, moved from lower Woodward to a new larger location on Monroe. Many famous entertainers and magicians made Detroit a regular stop.

Ransom E. Olds and his investors established the first factory in Detroit and the country to manufacture automobiles. Olds and a partner were experimenting in Lansing for a couple of years but had a falling out, and Olds found new backing in Detroit. The Olds Motor Works was located in a small factory on the east side of Concord near Jefferson, near the Belle Isle bridge where the Uniroyal plant stood in later years.

Also in 1899, Mayor William Maybury and a couple of well-heeled pals raised $15,000 to help Henry Ford form the Detroit Automobile Company. Ford became chief engineer and partner and quit his job at Edison.

While Olds and Ford were beginning their rise to fame and fortune, the end of the century brought an end to one of Detroit's legends. Hiram Walker, who tried several unsuccessful business ventures in Detroit before opening a grocery store on Woodward and going into the whiskey business on the other side of the river in 1858, died at the age of 82.

Looking west from City Hall as the century ended.

1900-1909

As the twentieth century dawned, the greater Detroit area had 304,132 residents. The city's population of 285,704 made the city the nation's 13th largest. Almost 12 percent couldn't speak English and many were employed in Detroit's stove factories and breweries. A half-century after Bernhard Stroh opened his small brewery, Stroh's was the largest of Detroit's 23 beer producers.

City Hall was decorated for Detroit's bicentennial in 1901. (MV)

It was a new time for the electric trolley cars that rolled on the city's main thoroughfares. All streetcar lines were united into one system: the Detroit United Railway. The more comfortable, plush Interurbans made 330 daily runs from the station at Jefferson and Bates to the far-flung suburbs and points beyond.

In 1901 Roy Chapin drove an Oldsmobile from Detroit to New York for America's first auto show. Chapin made the trip in seven and a half days. The journey was a financial success for Ransom Olds, who gained hundreds of new customers.

Master mechanics John and Horace Dodge won a contract to supply a thousand engines to the Olds Motor Works, but a fire destroyed the Olds plant and all the production plans and machinery. It was back to the drawing board as only a small experimental model with a curved dash was salvaged, and Olds decided to start over back in Lansing.

The Henry Ford Automobile Company was formed but Ford soon dropped out and the company was dissolved. The Cadillac Company was incorporated as many auto related companies arrived and departed.

At the turn of the century, Detroit's baseball franchise was in the Western League, which was renamed the American League. In 1901 the American League was granted equal status with the National League and the two leagues were considered major leagues.

Fans always checked the roof of the Hammond Building during baseball season to see if a white flag with a blue circle was flying, as it meant the Tigers would be in action at Bennett Park. The Tigers drew the largest baseball crowd ever in the city, 10,023, for the 1901 home opener. Many left in disgust as the Tigers were on the wrong end of a 13-4 score in the ninth inning. Those who stayed were rewarded as Detroit scored 10 times in the bottom of the ninth for a 14-13 victory.

Seven weeks later Hazen Pingree died at age 60. The popular politician's casket was brought to the main corridor of the City Hall and wreaths were placed on the exterior of the building. A long line of silent mourners extended for six blocks and filed past the bier for the rest of the day and the day after.

A little more than two weeks after Pingree's burial on July 24, Detroit held an elaborate celebration to mark the city's bicentennial. Parades of celebrants

Cadillac Square from the Wayne County Building, looking west to City Hall in 1906. The Majestic Building is on the right at the corner of Woodward and Michigan.

Above: The impressive Wayne County Building opened in 1902 at Cadillac Square and Randolph. (IC)

Left: Detroiter Edward Wagner is credited with the carved ornamentation, cherubs, and wreaths above windows, and the figures including General Anthony Wayne and Indians concluding a peace treaty. (IC)

Right: New York sculptor John Massey Rhind created the bronze quadrigas representing Victory and Progress. (JF)

and shoppers occupied the business district and all kinds of automobiles were seen and heard.

In 1902 Jefferson and Brush was the hub of automobile row—there were four dealerships near the corner. Detroit held its first auto show and a few months later had its first auto accident fatality when well-heeled lumberman George Bissell's carriage was hit at Brooklyn and Lysander.

There were 44 millionaires in town in 1902, while carpenters proposed a minimum wage of thirty cents hourly and house painters asked for $2.50 a day.

Almost five years after the cornerstone was laid in October 1897, the impressive Wayne County Building was dedicated and many employees moved east across Cadillac Square from the City Hall.

David Buick stumbled upon the idea of the valve-in-head motor in 1903. His Buick Company was purchased by former carriage maker William Durant, who planned a combination of automobiles that would eventually become General Motors. Meanwhile, the new Packard plant—designed by Albert Kahn—became the world's first reinforced concrete factory.

The Ford Motor Company was incorporated in June 1903. The Dodge brothers supplied Ford with transmissions, engines, and axles. Ford's factory was located at Bellevue and Mack, and 40-year-old Henry Ford owned 25 percent of the stock. One of the investors was James Couzens, who mortgaged his house to come up with the $2,000 needed to be part of the new company.

Earlier in the year, Ford's old employer, the Edison Illuminating Company, became Detroit Edison with 220 employees. All of Detroit's employees were affected by the price of milk in 1903, as it was raised to seven cents a quart.

In 1904 Ford Motor had fewer than 40 employees, and Jonathan Maxwell, a former factory manager for Olds, teamed up with Benjamin Briscoe to produce the Maxwell car from a factory at Jefferson near Connors.

Albert Kahn designed a factory of a different kind for the Burroughs Adding Machine Company on Second Avenue. William Burroughs, inventor and founder, had died six years earlier in 1898, and the new company president felt Detroit presented a better climate than St. Louis for growth and profits.

Memories of former mayor and governor Hazen Pingree abounded on Memorial Day as a statue was unveiled in Grand Circus Park at Woodward and Adams. Later that summer, Belle Isle had another attraction for visitors as the Aquarium opened.

In 1905 Michigan law required automobile drivers to pull over and stop if approaching horses appeared spooked by their machine. Movies were becoming more popular. The "Casino," Detroit's first theater built exclusively for the showing of movies, opened on Monroe.

Sixty-two years after his death in New York from pneumonia at the age of 31 in 1842, the remains of Governor Stevens T. Mason were brought to Detroit and interred in Capitol Park. Plans were made for a monument and bronze statue of Mason that would be placed above his final resting place.

Eighteen-year-old Tyrus Cobb was on a train headed to Detroit. Cobb's baseball contract was purchased from the minor league Augusta club for $700 by Tigers management. Cobb arrived at Michigan Central on Tuesday night August 30, 1905, with his little fielder's glove, three bats, and articles of clothing. No one met him, so Cobb hired a horse-drawn

Ty Cobb was 18 when he made his major league debut with the Tigers in 1905.

The old Belle Isle Bridge saw a lot of traffic in the early 1900s. A manacled Harry Houdini gained publicity by jumping off it in 1906. (MV)

cab and found a cheap hotel near Bennett Park.

Cobb woke up in a different world. People didn't talk the way he was used to and spoke languages he had never heard. But he was playing in the major leagues and signed a contract calling for $1,500. Twenty years later Cobb would still be playing for the Tigers and would be a millionaire.

In 1906 the Michigan State Telephone Company (the future Michigan Bell) had almost 100,000 customers and published the country's first classified business yellow pages. Prices of food edged up as a dozen eggs cost twenty-six cents and a loaf of bread was seven cents. Henry Ford bought out some investors to claim 51 percent of Ford Motor and moved his automobile operations to a larger plant on Piquette near Beaubien.

Between rave appearances at the Temple Theater, 32-year-old Harry Houdini drew a lot of attention and Detroiters to the Belle Isle Bridge on a November afternoon. The manacled magician jumped from the bridge into the depths of the cold Detroit River while spectators held their breath. Minutes later Houdini appeared through the splashy waters

and swam to a waiting lifeboat, displaying the open cuffs.

New residents kept coming in 1907 and there were plenty of employment opportunities as the railroad car industry was at its peak in Detroit and had about 9,000 workers. The auto industry had more competition and opportunity for employment as Charles B. King organized his own company. King designed the first automobile with the steering wheel on the left side and would produce autos using his many innovations.

Automobile Row, along Jefferson on both sides of Brush, had 16 dealers in 1907. More autos meant more accidents, and Detroit had seven auto fatalities, prompting police to try to enforce an auto speed limit of eight miles per hour downtown and 12 miles per hour in residential areas. There was talk of replacing steam fire engines with motorized apparatus, and talk became fact when the fire chief had the fire department's first automobile.

The lavish Hotel Pontchartrain opened at the site of the old Russell House on Woodward and Cadillac Square. A short walk up Woodward, Sebastian

Spering Kresge became sole owner of his "dime store." On Cass Avenue, Lewis Cass Technical High School became the city's first high school to be named for an individual.

Ninety-four-year-old Emily Mason, sister of former Governor Stevens T. Mason, came back to town in 1908 for the Memorial Day unveiling of her brother's monument in Capitol Park, where his remains had been interred three years earlier.

Automobile taxicabs with automatic fare registers made their Detroit debut in 1908. Detroit wasn't yet the auto capital of the world, but the industry kept growing locally as Ford Motor produced its first Model T, which sold for $950. William Durant founded General Motors around the Buick and Oldsmobile Companies.

Hudson's and Kern's had competition nearby as the Crowley, Milner & Company was founded and took over a store at Gratiot and Farmer. A growing city meant more garbage and the city council passed an ordinance providing Detroiters with regular trash collection.

William Maybury, who held several political offices including mayor of Detroit, died in 1909. Maybury was widely admired and citizens quickly raised funds to erect a statue in his memory on the east side of Woodward at Adams.

Automobiles were getting heavier, going faster, and being driven further. The first mile of concrete paved road in the country opened on Woodward from Six Mile to Seven Mile roads. Roy Chapin, who may have driven more miles than anyone by 1909 in his role as chief test driver for Olds, became president of the newly organized Hudson Motor Car Company.

The Tigers won their third straight American League pennant and lost their third straight World Series. One of the games at Bennett Park drew a record crowd for Detroit baseball of 18,277.

The remains of Stevens T. Mason were interred in Capitol Park in 1905. This monument was placed above his final resting place in 1908. (IC)

1910-1919

Detroit's 1910 population of 465,766 included 5,741 black residents and 157,534 who were foreign born. The Highland Park Plant of Ford Motor began operation. There were 201 other makes of cars produced by an estimated 150 companies. Many were displayed at the Detroit Auto Show, held at the Wayne Gardens at Third and Jefferson.

Lumber baron David Whitney died in 1910, leaving a fortune estimated at $15 million and several properties, including the five-floor Grand Circus Park Building on Woodward and Park. A bit farther north on Woodward at Montcalm, Fred Hughes and Leslie Hatcher opened a fine men's clothing store. The two friends called it Hughes and Hatcher.

Foul-mouthed Jim Scott, Detroit's meanest man, died at the age of 79. People crossed the street to avoid him. Scott had a reputation of hanging around bars and ladies of ill repute, insulting people, and

City Hall, Dime Savings Bank and Majestic Building, Detroit, Mich.

P-1358

Detroiters marveled at the city's tallest building as the Dime Building opened on Griswold in 1910.

buying property next to someone he didn't like. Scott, who inherited his father's real estate fortune at a young age, would overpay for property just to put a billboard on the roof to block out the sun and view of someone he didn't care for.

Scott was 45 when he married in 1876 and seemed to enjoy marriage and respectability. He was seen going to church weekly and at all the right places. However, when he died 34 years after his marriage, Scott was remembered for his pre-marriage days. His will leaving property "to the City of Detroit to build a fountain on Belle Isle to be called the James Scott Fountain" sparked debate among politicians, newspapermen, and Detroiters of all ages and dominated the news in 1910. Department store owner J.L. Hudson, who carried a lot of weight around town, summed up his feelings on the sub-ject: "Mr. Scott never did anything for Detroit in his lifetime and he never had a thought that was good for the city." Most movers and shakers agreed with Hudson, but Scott's defenders would wait for the controversy to die down a bit.

Michigan Central Railroad began using the tunnel under the Detroit River for freight and passenger trains. Above ground, Detroit's first flight occurred when pilot Arch Hoxsey flew his biplane at the Fairgrounds. About two weeks later on the first of August, the Jessie Bonstelle Stock Company opened its first theatrical season at the Garrick Theater on Griswold.

Racing driver Louis Chevrolet developed a six-cylinder car ready for production in 1911, financed by William Durant. A few cars were produced at a rented plant on West Grand Boulevard and the

The Michigan Central Railroad Station featured a five-story domed ceiling over the waiting room. (MV)

Chevrolet Motor Company was organized.

Up Woodward at a former 60-acre racetrack in Highland Park, Ford Motor turned out 34,500 Model T's. Downriver in Trenton, Wayne County Road Commissioner Edward Hines directed the painting of the world's first white center line on a roadway.

The Albert Kahn-designed National Theater opened on Monroe for vaudeville and the Detroit Zoological Society was organized.

Detroit went over the half million population mark in 1912 and Michigan produced more cars than any other state. Ford more than doubled its produc-tion from the previous year as 78,440 Model T's came off the lines, while Chevrolet turned out 2,999 cars in its first full year.

Walter Chrysler, the master locomotive me-chanic, was hired to manage Buick's production ,and Cadillac made big news when it adopted the self-starter as standard equipment. Joseph Lowthian Hudson, one of Detroit's most eligible bachelors, died, and his four nephews took over management of the city's largest department store.

Tigers owner Frank Navin had wooden Bennett Park torn down and moved the infield to the former

In 1914 David Charles Whitney had the Grand Circus Park Building razed and the David Whitney Building, named for his late lumber baron father, rose on the site.

Monroe Avenue in 1915 was the place to go for movies and vaudeville. The National Theatre, designed by Albert Kahn, was topped by a large clown and a sign. The Ste. Claire Hotel, looming in the distance at Monroe and Randolph, had been built in 1892. (MV)

left field area. The new one-decked concrete-and-steel structure had a capacity of 23,000.

Fans overwhelmingly wanted the same name for the new park, but politicians James Vernor (famous for his ginger ale) and John C. Lodge backed a council resolution calling for the "magnificent new ballpark be named Navin Field," to honor the team's owner who brought winning baseball and a fine facility to the city.

Navin Field had a great opening as over 24,000 squeezed into its yellow seats and poured onto the roped-off section of the field to watch the Tigers win 6-5 in 11 innings.

Frederick Sanders, who had founded his confectionery and ice cream store 38 years earlier, died in 1913. As older businessmen began to pass from the scene, Henry Ford initiated the assembly line in his Highland Park plant. Model T's could now be produced in 93 minutes instead of just over 12 hours. John Dodge left his post as a director of Ford Motor to join his brother Horace in their own automobile line.

The impressive Michigan Central Railroad Station opened on December 26, 1913. A two-story entrance hall topped by a 14-story office building became part of the West Side skyline. Visitors marveled at the 230-foot-long waiting room and craned their necks at the domed ceiling five stories above.

Thousands of men shivered in the early morning near-zero winds on January 14, 1914, at Ford's Highland Park plant. A few hours later the cold crowd of job-seekers swelled to 12,000. Ford promised five dollars daily for an eight-hour shift, slicing an hour off the work day for almost double the money. The combination of jobs and money made Detroit a magnet. Fourteen thousand applied by mail, and many left homes and farms in all parts of the country and even other countries.

The Dodge brothers were getting rave reviews for an automobile with an all-steel body coming off the lines at their 20-acre Hamtramck plant. Neighbors on East Boston Boulevard often saw John and Horace Dodge proudly sitting in the automobile bearing their name.

Ellsworth M. Statler, owner of the hotel chain, opened Detroit's fanciest hotel in February of 1915. The 800-room Statler faced Grand Circus Park on the site of former Governor John J. Bagley's home. Young Milton Statler, son of the owner, was lifted to the desk to be first to sign the register.

Detroiters were able to call San Francisco for the first time. It was extremely expensive as a 30-minute setup time was needed and customers weren't happy with the $16.70 charge for three minutes.

Henry Ford was a proud man in 1915 as his company produced a million Model T's. (MV)

Two of Detroit's papers—the *News* and the *Journal*—merged in 1915. Detroiters were saddened to read of the burning of the Belle Isle Bridge on April 27.

While Henry Ford built a million Model T's in 1915, Roy Fruehauf and his son Harvey gave birth to the first modern truck trailer as their vehicle with hard rubber tires and flat sides made its debut.

The elegant Detroit Athletic Club opened on Madison Avenue in 1915. Albert Kahn, who designed the building, refused an invitation to the first luncheon to protest the club's policy of barring Jews from membership.

In 1916 you could buy a Ford for $440 or the most expensive model for $975. Ford Motor produced half of America's automobiles and 40 percent of the world's.

A popular auto among women was the Detroit Electric. It was priced from $2,125 to $2,775 and could run from 80 to 100 miles on a single battery charge. Unlike nonelectric models, cranking and shifting weren't needed, making them ideal for women.

Detroit's black population reached 8,000 in 1916. The city had its first registered Girl Scout troop and the Albert Kahn-designed Detroit News Building opened on Lafayette.

Ford produced its first truck in 1917, and more cars were seen in the streets. To relieve congestion, Mayor Oscar Marx promoted the idea of a subway, while the *Free Press* suggested an elevated monorail system.

To help direct traffic, the city installed an elevated platform supporting a policeman responsible for regulating traffic flow on Woodward Avenue. It provided a sense of security for pedestrians and reduced reckless driving.

On June 5, 1917, two months after the United States entered World War I, Detroit's males between the ages of 21 and 30 had to register for the draft. Fort Wayne saw action by housing battalions of troops, and 65,000 of the city's men and women would serve in the armed forces.

Despite the two-cent fare increase to five cents,

Left: The Warren Avenue streetcar makes its way to the Michigan Central Railroad Station on Michigan Avenue in 1916. (MV)

Below: The first elevated traffic control tower made its debut on Woodward Avenue in 1917. (MV)

the Grand Circus Park area became a more popular destination for streetcar riders, as the Madison and Adams theaters were in operation.

Richard H. Fyfe built Detroit's tallest shoe store at the northwest corner of Adams and Woodward in 1918. The last of the city's electric arc light towers were removed that year.

Edsel Ford, Henry's son, became president of Ford Motor and production began at the Rouge plant. Detroit's working people objected to the penny streetcar fare increase as the weekly round trips added up.

In May of 1918, about 200,000 women in Wayne County over the age of 16 registered for war work. Because of the war, jobs previously held by men were available, and women became streetcar conductors and letter carriers.

The present city charter went into effect in 1918. The ward system was abolished and the elected nine-man Common Council was adopted. Seventy-year-old James Vernor was the oldest councilman. The Fort Shelby Hotel opened on the historic corner where the fort once stood and the price of eggs rose to 65 cents a dozen.

Thousands swarmed to Campus Martius to celebrate the end of the war on November 11. The festivities were tempered by the fact that 1,360 Detroiters were killed serving their country.

A Spanish flu epidemic ravaged the city over the winter. Theaters, schools and even churches were closed. Hundreds died, and thousands seeking protection from the flu donned gauze face masks.

James Couzens, one of Henry Ford's early partners, sold his Ford stock for over $29 million in

Looking south down Woodward from the top of the Majestic Building. The Pontchartrain Hotel at Cadillac Square and Woodward was in its last year of operation in 1919. (MV)

Over 2,000 attended the opening of Orchestra Hall on October 23, 1919. (IC)

1919. Besides becoming one of the city's wealthiest men, Couzens became mayor of Detroit.

Detroit's five largest stove companies employed almost 5,000 workers in 1919 and the Kern department store at Woodward and Gratiot was rebuilt and modernized.

The Detroit Stars of the Negro National League began playing their games at Mack Park. The shabby little wooden ballpark had 6,000 seats and was located on Mack and Fairview.

Five years after Weston Gales led the Detroit Orchestra in concert at the Detroit Opera House, marking the beginning of the Detroit Symphony, Ossip Gabrilowitsch, internationally known Russian pianist, moved to Detroit as conductor of the Detroit Symphony Orchestra. Gabrilowitsch was married to soprano Clara Clemens, the daughter of Mark Twain. Gabrilowitsch urged the building of Orchestra Hall and led the DSO on opening night, October 23, 1919, before a packed house of 2,018.

1920-1929

In 1920 Detroit's population of 993,678 was ranked fourth in the nation. In only 20 years the population had increased by over 700,000, and in ten years the population had increased by about 528,000. 290,884 of Detroit's 1920 residents were foreign born. Because of anti-Jewish violence in Eastern Europe, many Jews came to America and settled in Detroit. While Detroit's population increased by 114 percent in ten years, the Jewish population had a 247 percent increase, to 3.7 percent of the city's total. The black population grew by 611 percent in only ten years, from 5,741 to 40,838, or 4.1 percent of Detroit's 1920 total.

Because of the Ford plant, Highland Park went from 4,120 residents in 1910 to 46,499 only 10 years later.

The cornerstone for the world's largest Masonic Temple was laid in 1920 opposite Cass Park.

A symbolic ceremony was held in River Rouge on May 17, 1920, as Edsel Ford's three-year-old son Henry, safely held in his grandfather's arms, lit the famous Rouge Blast Furnace, ushering in the further growth of the company and creating thousands of new jobs.

Thousands admired Henry Ford and thousands didn't. Starting in 1920, Ford used his *Dearborn Independent* newspaper to blame Jews for the country's social and economic problems. Besides being sold on the street, the paper reached all corners of the country, as all Ford agencies carried the publication.

Above: The Albert Kahn-designed General Motors Building was completed in 1921.

Below: World War I delayed the opening and tripled construction costs for the Main Library.

Detroit policeman William Potts developed the multicolored traffic signal. The first was installed at Woodward and Fort in 1920, while this one on Woodward at Congress made its debut in 1922. This view is from Congress looking north on Woodward. (MV)

In 1920 there were two horses for every car in the country, and William Durant was forced out as head of General Motors. Walter Chrysler left his executive vice president post at GM to become president of the Maxwell Chalmers Motor Car Company. John and Horace Dodge died months apart from influenza. Factory workers served as pallbearers and the inseparable brothers were buried next to each other at Woodlawn Cemetery.

To help move more people, the Detroit Motorbus Company had eight doubledecked buses operating on some of the city's busy streets. By August airmail deliveries between Detroit and Cleveland began.

Radio began August 20, 1920, from a room on the second floor of the Detroit News Building on Lafayette and Second. A transmission operator and technical aide had a phonograph and a couple of records. The phonograph was placed next to the transmitter and the operator, Frank Edwards, leaned over the microphone and announced. "This is 8MK calling." (The station wouldn't be called WWJ until 1922). The phonograph began to play "Roses of Picardy" and history was made as about a hundred ham operators heard the world's first radio station through the night air.

Women felt more liberated in the new decade as

they voted for the first time in a general primary election, after also serving as jurors for the first time the previous year in county courts.

The white Vermont marble Italian Renaissance style Main Library opened on Woodward at Kirby in 1921. The General Motors Building was completed and Cadillac Motor Company consolidated its operations into its new Clark Street facility.

Assembly line mass production reduced the price of Model T's from $850 in 1908 to $260 in 1921. The Detroit Police Department boasted it had the world's first radio equipped car, a Model A Ford, to help patrol the streets.

The Agricultural Society gave the state of Michigan 164 acres on the east side of Woodward south of Eight Mile Road to house the annual Michigan State Fair. The acreage had been bought by Joseph L. Hudson 16 years earlier and deeded to the Agricultural Society.

The Detroit Fire Department was entirely motorized by 1922 and the police department had several radio equipped cars to receive messages. WWJ had two wires extended 290 feet to the Fort Shelby Hotel, increasing its broadcast range. On February 15, 1922, Ossip Gabrilowitsch, the Detroit Symphony Orchestra, and WWJ teamed up to broadcast

and CBS furnished hours of programming.

After obtaining advertising sponsors and paying CBS, Trendle felt he could be more profitable by going independent and coming up with his own programming. There were the usual bands and singers, but Trendle wanted to create something different for listeners. He wanted heroes who would appeal to all ages. Dramas would be cheap to produce, as they didn't require famous actors and could be produced using staff from the already-successful WXYZ show, "Warner Lester Manhunter." Trendle tossed around ideas for weeks with station director Jim Jewell in the offices of WXYZ. Jewell narrowed down the new hero to a Texas Ranger who had survived an ambush. After a little more fine tuning, the Lone Ranger was born.

Jewell added some final touches spiced with personal memories. His father-in-law owned a boys camp at Mullet Lake, Michigan, called "Kee Mo Sah Bee," which Jewell fast-forwarded a bit to "Kemo Sabe." Jewell also recalled an Indian around the camp with a drinking problem. When he drank, other Indians called him "a Tonto." While it was not a kind name to call someone with a drinking problem, it had a nice ring to it.

Jewell presented Trendle with the idea of giving the Lone Ranger an Indian companion named Tonto who called his friend Kemo Sabe, an Indian term for trusted friend. Trendle, Jewell. and WXYZ staffers came up with the idea of the Ranger wearing a mask fashioned from the vest of his ambushed brother. All that was needed now was to find a good script writer to do justice to WXYZ's masked rider of the plains.

Trendle, familiar with the writing talents of Fran Striker who operated from his home in Buffalo, New York, offered Striker the job of writing scripts provided he followed the rules—the Lone Ranger never killed anyone and shot silver bullets only to disarm outlaws he turned over to the proper authorities.

Detroiter George Stenius, who had local acting experience with the Jesse Bonstelle players, won the audition to be the radio voice of the Lone Ranger. Stenius held the job only briefly, as he had higher show business aspirations. He moved to Hollywood, changed his name to George Seaton, worked on Marx Brothers films, and gained fame as a writer-director and producer. Later Seaton would win an Oscar for *Miracle on 34th Street* and *The Country Girl*.

Meanwhile, back at the studio, the Lone Ranger was heard in Michigan three times a week. Audiences responded enthusiastically to the voice of Earle W. Graser as the masked man. Graser, who took drama at nearby City College (soon to be renamed Wayne University), was young, slim, and of average height with a full head of black hair and pencil-thin mustache. Audiences, though, heard a deep, vibrant, and commanding voice and pictured the Lone Ranger.

The only man to ever play the role of Tonto on the radio was John Todd. A Detroiter with Shakespearean acting experience, Todd taught drama in Detroit's Conservatory of Arts and was the voice of other WXYZ characters. However, he would be Tonto for the entire radio run of the Lone Ranger.

In July 1933, about six months after the first Lone Ranger episode aired, Detroit's Department of Recreation held its annual field day on Belle Isle. It was advertised that the Lone Ranger would appear, but Trendle didn't send Earle Graser because he was unathletic looking. Instead station announcer Brace Beemer, a tall man with a deep voice and an expert horseman, would ride a white horse called Silver.

The masked man made an appearance during the children's circus and galloped around the arena where 10,000 people were squeezed together. As he started to ride away, spectators, clowns, and other performers formed the biggest posse Detroit had ever seen and went after the radio hero, hoping for a closer look. Sensing the stampede, Beemer yelled to the oncoming crowd, "Back, you rangers; back to your posts!" Months of rehearsal went for naught as the last acts of the circus and the final march by school bands never took place. Trendle was pleased at the crowd but afraid of what might happen next time the Lone Ranger went out in public. He confined the hero to the WXYZ studio on the top floors of the Maccabees Buildings with Earle Graser con-

Walter O. Briggs beamed as all-star catcher and manager Mickey Cochrane led the Tigers to the World Series in his first season in Detroit. (photo courtesy Detroit Tigers)

tinuing to play the lead role.

Trendle wondered about the actual size of the listening audience in Michigan. He devised an offer for a free Lone Ranger popgun, but only to the first 300 listeners writing in. Mailbags poured in and 24,905 pieces of mail were counted. Trendle had the piles of mail photographed with Mayor Frank Couzens and Postmaster Roscoe Huston and shopped it around to potential sponsors. Scriptwriter Fran Striker moved to Detroit and settled in on Chalmers near the Detroit River. With proof of the program's popularity, a sponsor was lined up by November. By 1934, stations in Chicago, New York, and Cincinnati carried the Lone Ranger, and Trendle helped form the Mutual Radio Network to spur further growth and profits.

Also in 1934, various colleges merged into one university named Wayne University, and the imposing Federal Building and Post Office filling an entire block opened on Lafayette.

The main topic of conversation among men returning to work as the Depression eased was sports. The hockey club that had come to town eight years earlier as the Cougars was renamed the Falcons in 1930 and the Red Wings in 1932. The Wings were putting on a good show at seven-year-old Olympia and drawing more fans and interest.

A pro football team soon followed as the Portsmouth, Ohio, Spartans were purchased for $15,000 and renamed the Lions. The team played at the University of Detroit stadium and won its first 10 games.

The Tigers, under new manager Mickey

Cochrane, won their first American League pennant in 25 years. Team president and owner Frank Navin had bought Cochrane from Philadelphia the previous winter, as owner Connie Mack was selling players to pay bills brought on by the Depression. To pay Mack's asking price of $100,000 for the All-Star catcher, Navin, also hurt by the economic collapse, turned to co-owner Walter O. Briggs for money. Briggs, who had bought a quarter ownership in 1920 and another quarter seven years later, lent the club the amount needed to acquire Cochrane. Cochrane agreed to manage the Tigers and to act as starting catcher, and he excelled in both roles.

However, a happy ending to the 1934 season was denied when the St. Louis Cardinals crushed the Tigers in the seventh game of the World Series 11-0 at Navin Field. The Tigers drew 919,161 paying customers during the season, 598,189 more than in

Dapper Frank Navin checks out the goings-on at Navin Field. (BHC)

1933. The Cardinals, sharing St. Louis with the American League's Browns, only drew 335,000 in 1934. The Cardinals, made up of a colorful cast of characters with nicknames like Dizzy, Daffy, Ducky, Pepper, and others, looked for greener pastures. Cardinals executive Branch Rickey, with approval from club owner Sam Breadon, tried to move the team to Detroit and rent Navin Field. Navin and Briggs turned the offer down, probably fearing the colorful Cardinals—known as the Gashouse Gang—would be a more popular draw than the Tigers.

Detroit was the city of champions in 1935 as all three of the city's professional teams won titles. The Tigers defeated the Chicago Cubs in the World Series that fall, and fans poured out of Navin Field in celebration. Police estimated a half million revelers joined in, and soon Woodward was a solid line of cars with horns blowing. Pedestrians added to the din by clanging garbage can covers. Frank Navin, known as Old Poker Face, smiled all the way to his home on Longfellow, a few doors west of Woodward.

Scarcely a month later, Navin, still basking in his first World Series victory in three decades of ownership, relaxed by going horseback riding on Belle Isle, one of his favorite activities. The riderless horse returned to the stables, prompting a search party effort. Navin's body was found in the woods and rushed to Detroit Osteopathic Hospital in Highland Park, where he was pronounced dead of a heart attack. Walter O. Briggs purchased the 50 percent stock that Navin held and became sole owner of the team and Navin Field.

Ossip Gabrilowitsch died in 1936. He had begun conducting the Detroit Symphony Orchestra in 1918 and conducted radio's first complete symphony on WWJ in 1922. Gabrilowitsch created a weekly symphony program for radio in 1934 that went national months before his death.

Three hundred sixty-four Detroiters died in a July heat wave as the thermometer topped 100 for seven consecutive days. Mounted policemen poured buckets of water on their horses and people wore cabbage leaves on their heads as they sought relief from the heat.

The heat was turned up on the Black Legion in 1936. Thought responsible for at least 50 killings in the area in the past five years, investigators estimated that the Black Legion, which began as the elite "Black Guard" of the Ku Klux Klan, had more than 24,000 active Night Riders willing to commit violence and murder. Members included police and political officials. They did their dirty work under the cover of darkness and white sheets. When the investigative spotlight was turned on, the sheets came off and they blended in with Detroit's white citizenry. They didn't completely go away, though. They made their national headquarters in Detroit in 1937, called themselves the United Brotherhood of America, and specialized in anti-union activities.

After a three-month strike at General Motors and a one-month strike at Chrysler, the two companies recognized the United Auto Workers union. With agreements at Hudson Motor, Packard, Studebaker, and some parts companies, Ford was the UAW's next target. On May 26, 1937, Walter Reuther, a former Ford assembly line worker who became a UAW organizer, had a legal permit to distribute leaflets outside the Ford Rouge Plant in Dearborn. Henry Ford was vehemently opposed to union recognition and allowed his hatchet man, Harry Bennett, to bolster security. Bennett hired former wrestlers and known hoodlums to stand guard at plant gates. As Reuther, Richard Frankenstein, and a few union associates got ready to distribute their leaflets, they were ordered to leave. With tough-looking men approaching, Reuther and his party complied, but their exit was blocked by more of Bennett's men. The union men were rushed, beaten, kicked, and stomped by Bennett's thugs.

Photographers caught the violence on film and raced away before Bennett's gang—which also included some Dearborn policemen—could get at

While Detroiters listened to the radio in 1937, reading was the most popular way to keep up with current events. Downtown Detroit had seven outdoor newsstands. Sam Kugel managed this stand on the north side of Michigan Avenue at the west side of Griswold. (photo courtesy Triangle News Co.)

Joe Louis, an avid Tigers fan, fought at Briggs Stadium in 1939. (BHC)

them and their cameras. When the photographs appeared in the papers, the union gained sympathy and public opinion turned against Ford. Because of Bennett's bloody blunder in what became known as the Battle of the Overpass, union membership picked up. By July 1937 the UAW had 200,000 members in Detroit and 370,000 nationwide.

The Lone Ranger went national in 1937 via the WXYZ studios in the Maccabees Building. Earle W. Graser, who had assumed the role of the masked rider of the plains in 1933, continued to bring outlaws to justice. Going nationwide meant the programs, which aired Monday, Wednesday and Friday at 7:30 p.m., had to be performed twice more on those nights for the different time zones. The hardworking cast, which at times included actor John Hodiak and entertainer Danny Thomas, had to do three live shows three times a week.

Most residents on Auburn Street between Midland and Fenkell had no idea that the quiet, unassuming Graser lived on the block. At times an elderly bald man sporting a bow tie would visit. John Todd and Earle Graser were as close as the Lone Ranger and Tonto roles they played on the air. Despite the difference in their ages, they enjoyed each other's company and often played cards together.

Variety, the noted theatrical weekly newspaper, honored WXYZ with the 1937 Showmanship Award for the country's most successful radio station in creating popular programs. "The Green Hornet" also became a popular national show, and "Children's Theatre of the Air" was very popular with younger listeners. The musical comedy was presented entirely by children ages five to 14. The 45-minute show came from the stage of the Broadway Capitol (now the Michigan Opera House) each Sunday afternoon.

Joe Louis, who came out of Detroit's Brewster Recreation Center, won the world's heavyweight boxing championship by defeating James Braddock. Charles Ward, *Free Press* sports editor, dubbed Louis "The Brown Bomber." The Red Wings were skating to a second Stanley Cup in two years, and construction to entirely double deck the Tigers' ballpark was almost complete.

Father Charles Coughlin began radio sermons on WJR in 1926. By 1933, the "Radio Priest" had his own network of stations as he bought time with listener contributions. In 1936 listeners noticed a shift in Coughlin's ideas. Previously a supporter of labor unions and President Roosevelt, the priest from Royal Oak's Shrine of the Little Flower often criticized both. Coughlin brazenly called Roosevelt the "great betrayer and liar." By 1937, more church superiors openly rebuked Coughlin and his rhetoric. In 1938 more Catholics in positions other than in the church criticized Coughlin and his opinions. Coughlin responded by becoming more defiant and offended even more people by delivering openly anti-Semitic broadcasts. While Hitler called for violence against Jews in broadcasts heard in Europe, Coughlin told his audience that Hitler stood as a "defense mechanism against the incursions of communism."

Coughlin continued his support of Hitler and anti-Jewish tirades, but most listeners were not in agreement and withdrew financial support.

Henry Ford celebrated his 75th birthday in 1938. Eyebrows were raised when Ford accepted the Grand Cross of the Supreme Order of the German Eagle, the Third Reich's highest honor for a non-German. The award, created by Hitler, was presented to Ford by the German consul and provoked a local and national reaction.

Hank Greenberg followed the activities of Coughlin and Ford with great interest. The Tigers All-Star first baseman often felt the sting of anti-Semitism on the baseball field as opposing players would shout remarks from the safety of their dugout, surrounded by their teammates. The 6-foot-4 Greenberg hit 40 home runs with an amazing 183 runs batted in while averaging .337 in 1937. In 1938 he hit 58 home runs, the first season Walter O. Briggs called the remodeled ballpark Briggs Stadium.

Some non-baseball-playing Greenbergs seeking jobs had to change their name to Green just to be considered for employment, as newspapers carried ads from Detroit employers seeking gentiles only.

Signs were seen on Detroit residential buildings stating, "No Dogs or Jews Allowed." With Hitler raging in Europe, Coughlin on the radio, some of Henry Ford's previously sponsored publications still in circulation, and anti-Semitism openly displayed in housing and employment, the Jewish community of Detroit found escapism and a hero in Greenberg's exploits on the baseball field.

While Greenberg was hitting home runs, Joe Louis pummeled German heavyweight Max Schmelling in the ring for boxing's highest rung. The black and Jewish communities were delirious as Detroit celebrated the defeat of the hope of Nazi Germany.

Louis was an avid Tigers fan and was often seen at games. On September 20, 1939, 33,000 boxing fans watched Louis retain the heavyweight championship of the world at Briggs Stadium. It was a rainy evening but the wet fans were rewarded when Louis knocked out challenger Bob Pastor in the eleventh round. Louis earned $118,000 for the fight, three times more than Greenberg, his favorite Tiger player, was paid for the 1939 season.

The Packard signs on East Grand Boulevard were close to the Packard plant. In 1939 Packard was the first company to offer air-conditioned cars. On Mt. Elliott, cars drove to the right of the tracks, as streetcars were 46 feet long and eight feet wide. (MV)

WORLD WAR II: 1940-1945

While buildings and families were being torn apart in war-ravaged Europe, Detroit prospered as many families moved to the motor city in search of a better economic life. Because of the Depression, Detroit had only grown by 3.5 percent in the past ten years.

Black residents numbered 149,119 or 9.2 percent of Detroit's 1940 population of 1,623,452. Many southern whites moved to Detroit for the same reason blacks did: jobs. Almost 20 percent of Detroit's population was foreign born and most were paying close attention to the events in Europe.

Detroiters were paying close attention to the Tigers as they won the American League pennant. Game five of the World Series played at Briggs Stadium drew 55,189 paying fans—a record at the time—and the fans went home happy as the Tigers won. However, the Tigers lost the next two games in Cincinnati and thus the World Series

Hank Greenberg was named the American League's Most Valuable Player in 1940. Greenberg, who hit .340 with 41 home runs and 150 RBIs, was looking forward to the 1941 All-Star Game scheduled for Briggs Stadium. Instead, the Tigers slugger became the first American League player to be drafted into the army that year and turned in his baseball uniform for an army one.

After eight years on WXYZ, the three-times-weekly Lone Ranger radio program was more popular than ever. Surveys indicated that 63 percent of the listening audience was made up of adults. Clark Griffith, the 72-year-old owner of the Washington Senators baseball team, made sure he was in his Griffith Stadium office near a radio on Lone Ranger nights even when his own team was playing on the field below. Clayton Moore, a 27-year-old actor and stunt man in Hollywood, had been an avid listener since the program went national. Moore had no idea at the time that George W. Trendle and Fran Striker would choose him to portray the masked man on a new invention called television before the decade was over.

The deep, authoritative, vibrant voice of Earle W. Graser was perfectly suited for the Lone Ranger. Graser sounded older than the 32 he turned on March 31, 1941. Few people outside of the WXYZ family got to know the gentle man who stayed out of the limelight. He preferred gardening and open spaces, which was why the Grasers moved to Farmington. The downside was the long trip from the studio home.

In the early hours of the morning on April 8, a drowsy Graser fell asleep at the wheel. As he passed the Methodist Church not far from his home, the car veered into a parked trailer, silencing one of the most popular radio voices in America.

America mourned. National publications from the *New York Times* to the *Los Angeles Times* carried obituaries and editorials. *Time* magazine called the Lone Ranger "the most adored character ever to be created on the U.S. air."

Staffers at WXYZ were stunned, as Graser had

been there the previous day giving voice to the Lone Ranger in the three usual rehearsals prior to the program, which ran in three time zones. George W. Trendle presided over a hastily called meeting. There wasn't much time, as the Lone Ranger was scheduled to gallop into America's homes the next night.

Trendle and his assistants went through the merits of the station's announcers. Mike Wallace was considered, as his voice was deep and sounded much older than his age, and because he did a good job narrating on The Green Hornet. (Yes, this was the same Mike Wallace who would be going strong six decades later on television's "Sixty Minutes.") However, Wallace's acting ability was questionable. Graser had been a fine actor with the Bonstelle Theater players and had also appeared in plays between scheduled movies at the Michigan Theater before joining WXYZ.

The list of candidates was narrowed to Brace Beemer, who at the time was narrating the Lone Ranger and doing the lead on "Challenge of the Yukon." He also had appeared in publicity photos and now would be able to do more public appearances. Best of all, his voice was similar to Graser's. To make the transition, it was decided that the masked man would be wounded and when the situation called for him to speak, it would be in a whisper for the next few programs.

The WXYZ staff took time out to attend Earle W. Graser's funeral, which was scheduled for April 10. Published reports claimed there were from 1,000 to 10,000 people lining Telegraph Road paying respects as the funeral cortege wound its way to the Grand Lawn cemetery entrance near Grand River.

When the Lone Ranger recovered from his wounds and Beemer was able to use his normal voice, it sounded like Graser's but with a head cold to some listeners. Beemer wasn't quite the actor that Graser had been and came across as more authoritative, less friendly.

Brace Beemer made more personal appearances after he assumed the radio role of the Lone Ranger in 1941. (BHC)

Beemer was an imposing figure. Well over six feet tall, he was an excellent horseman, a marksman with a pistol and rifle, and could hit the mark with a bullwhip as well. Beemer had no problem booming, "Hi-Yo, Silver" during the episode but couldn't handle the ending of the program, which called for "Hi-Yo, Silver, Away." The extra word didn't sound right to Trendle and the engineers, so they inserted a recording of Graser's "Hi-Yo, Silver, Away" at the end of each program.

Henry Ford couldn't make the UAW go away and finally signed an agreement with the union on April 10, 1941. Union persistence resulted in a 10-day strike before Ford capitulated. The UAW had kept public opinion on its side ever since the severe beating its leaders took by goons connected to Ford's security chief four years earlier.

Hudson's celebrated its 60th anniversary in 1941, and WWJ opened Michigan's first FM radio station in May, with studios at the top of the Penobscot Building.

Detroiters were following radio newscasts to monitor the situation in Europe and were shocked to hear that Japanese bombers had attacked Hawaii. The day after the bombing, December 8, 1941, the United States declared war on Japan and army guards were placed at the Ambassador Bridge and the Detroit-Windsor Tunnel. Regulations were imposed on the auto plants converted to production of war materials, and the "Motor City" became the "Arsenal of Democracy."

It was ironic that Albert Kahn, the son of a rabbi from Germany, designed many of the plants that shocked Hitler and his advisors with their production speed. Armored vehicles and aircraft engines and parts were rolling off the assembly lines.

Hank Greenberg, who was honorably discharged from the military service days before Pearl Harbor because Congress decided that men over 28 need not serve, became the first major leaguer to enlist in the Army. While he was excused from serving and offered a chance to stay stateside and be an athletic instructor, Greenberg elected to be a gunner in the

Hank Greenberg was a superstar in a baseball uniform and a hero in an army uniform. (photo courtesy Detroit Tigers)

Air Corps in the China-Burma-India Theater and rose to the rank of captain.

During the 1942 baseball season, the Tigers offered a 25-cent war stamp for every foul ball a fan returned. The balls would be sent to the troops overseas for recreational purposes. Radio play-by-play men were forbidden to mention weather conditions, as it was thought the information could aid the enemy in potential air attacks. Fans and players stood for the Star Spangled Banner prior to each game, instead of only on special occasions as in the past.

Catholic church superiors silenced Father Coughlin in 1942 and his magazine, *Social Justice*, was barred from the mail because of its stance on the United States war effort. in September, President Roosevelt visited Detroit's plants to check its war production. Roosevelt praised the efforts of the workers and the talents of architect Albert Kahn.

Less than three months after the president's visit, and a year and a day after the Japanese attack on Pearl Harbor, Albert Kahn died at the age of 73. The impressive monuments to Kahn's talent include the Fisher Building, the former General Motors Building, and numerous downtown structures.

Female riveters helped build B-24 bombers at the Willow Run plant. Rose Will Monroe, who played "Rosie the Riveter" during a national campaign to attract women to join the wartime workforce, was the most famous woman worker there. All 20,000 workers had an easier commute as the Willow Run Expressway (now I-94) opened its 24-mile stretch from Detroit to Willow Run. A much shorter stretch of the Davison Expressway had opened earlier in Highland Park.

Edsel Ford, who had been ailing during the war years, was only 49 when he died on May 26, 1943. Henry's only child was a talented designer and a generous humanitarian. Edsel and his son, Henry II, had tried to undo the damage the elder Ford did with his anti-Semitic publications. Edsel's lawyers had threatened the Ku Klux Klan with a lawsuit unless the Ford name was dropped from publications it was distributing. Because of the war, cars weren't being sold, but Edsel earmarked almost $84,000 for advertising in Jewish publications.

The war created more job opportunities at higher wages, and thousands of black families moved to Detroit in the year and a half since war was declared. Southern whites also joined the influx and competed for many of the same positions open to blacks.

The fires that raged within both groups couldn't be extinguished easily and added to the prejudice already reigning in the city. June 20, 1943, was a hot Sunday afternoon. Rumor fueled small incidents between blacks and whites. Each side heard that a woman and her baby of their color was thrown off the Belle Isle Bridge during a racial melee.

Mobs seeking to defend their side roamed the streets looking for trouble. Blacks struck first when an unsuspecting white pedestrian was beaten unconscious and run over by a taxicab. White owned stores were looted and motorists were pulled from their cars and severely beaten.

Gangs of whites took over Woodward Avenue downtown, pulling black people off streetcars and beating them. Blacks trying to escape the downtown mayhem by paying admission to movie theaters and hiding in the darkness weren't always successful. A

Six decades after his death, Albert Kahn is still Detroit's most famous architect. (BHC)

black man was found dead in a theater seat with six bullet wounds, and another seeking refuge in the Federal Building was beaten to death on its Fort Street steps.

Many blacks were beaten in the presence of police officers. Many were beaten by police officers. Many were killed by police officers. Police killed a total 17 people—all black.

On Monday night the first contingent of federal troops arrived. They made themselves visible and encamped on the vast lawn of the Public Library and various other public locations.

The violence produced 34 deaths and 676 injuries. Of the 1,838 arrested, 82 percent were black. It was time for Detroit's officials to take a hard look at the 3,400-man police force. The boys in blue were only slightly over one percent black.

Mayor Jeffries heard accounts of how lack of police intervention led to death and injury for blacks caught by white mobs during the riots. Sickened by reports of police standing by and watching while blacks were being beaten, and of strong action taken when the colors were reversed, Jeffries appointed an Interracial Relations Committee in January 1944.

In a 1944 national poll of radio writers in newspapers and magazines, the Lone Ranger placed first in popularity. The radio program's popularity spawned Lone Ranger badges, belts, books, bubble gum card sets, bracelets, clocks, coloring books, comic books, dust jackets for school books, first aid kits, funnies in national newspapers, hairbrushes, holsters, jigsaw puzzles, necklaces, novels, paint books, pennants, pencil boxes, printing sets, records, rings, schoolbags, silver bullets, slippers, thermos bottles, toothbrush holders, watches and, of course, masks.

The boys overseas didn't forget the Lone Ranger, either. The army often used trivia from the program as passwords, and pilots yelled, "Hi-Yo, Silver, Away," on takeoff. George W. Trendle, never one to miss an opportunity for a photo-op, arranged for Brace Beemer in full Lone Ranger regalia to bring Silver to the White House so the president's grandson could ride around the grounds. Trendle made sure he was close to FDR's grandson while the photographer clicked.

After eleven years, the Lone Ranger was still airing three times weekly on WXYZ. Other programs emanating from WXYZ over the national airwaves and doing well were "Challenge of the Yukon" and "The Green Hornet." John Todd, who played Tonto on the Lone Ranger, also played Inspector Conrad, Sergeant Preston's superior officer, and Dan Reid on the Green Hornet. Dan Reid was the Lone Ranger's nephew, and when the Hornet buzzed on the air, he was the father of Britt Reid, alias the Green Hornet, making the Lone Ranger the Green Hornet's great-uncle.

Thus Todd worked on three programs several times a week, as did other actors. Writers, announcers and actors at WXYZ numbered over 50, and George W. Trendle looked for larger quarters to house the ensemble. He purchased the large, stately mansion on Jefferson and Iroquois east of the Belle Isle Bridge. It was previously owned by Louis Mendelssohn, an architect, manufacturing draftsman, and businessman. The imposing three-story mansion, built in 1894, housed the entire WXYZ staff. The structure was dubbed the Lone Ranger Studios and the rooms were given appropriate names: the kitchen became Studio K, the drawing room was Studio D, and the garage was Studio G. Studio B—the bathroom—was always in use.

The best news of the decade was announced from New York on CBS by Bob Hite on August 14, 1945. Hite, a familiar voice to Detroiters as an announcer on the Lone Ranger and Green Hornet radio programs a few years earlier, was the first person on the radio with the bulletin that the war was over.

The boys were welcomed back with open arms. Hank Greenberg and Joe Louis were elevated to even higher hero status. Greenberg, a genuine battle hero who missed more than four baseball seasons, homered before a capacity crowd in his first game back.

Louis had his last pro fights in 1942 and donated those purses to the war effort before enlisting in the armed forces. The Army thought the heavyweight champion would be more valuable if he gave exhibitions to boost morale in U.S. bases around the world. Louis followed orders and fought 96 exhibitions before two million GIs in the United States, North Africa and Europe. Louis endeared himself to the American public when a reporter trying to elicit a comment asked, "Joe, we'll win because God is on our side, right?"

"No," Louis quickly responded, "We'll win because we're on God's side."

Downtown in 1945 was much the same as the wartime returnees remembered. Stores resumed pre-war hours the day after Labor Day. Monday hours were from 12 noon to 8:30 p.m. Tuesdays through Fridays were 9:30 a.m. to 5:30 p.m. on Saturdays the stores stayed open an extra half hour. Some specialty stores had daily hours of 9 a.m. to 9 p.m.

There were numerous stores catering to the tastes of men and women. Harry Suffrin's, a men's clothing establishment, had tweed suits for $25, and Kern's offered full-length fur coats for $89.

Labor Day 1945 moviegoers had a wealth of choices around Grand Circus Park. The Adams offered *A Thousand and One Nights,* starring Cornel Wilde, and *Boston Blackie's Rendezvous* with Chester Morris. There was an Abbott & Costello movie at the Fox, and a Charlie Chan adventure along with Bette Davis in *The Corn is Green* at the United Artists. Young couples went to see *Thrill of a Romance,* starring Van Johnson and Esther Williams, at the Michigan, while John Wayne lovers flocked to the Palms-State to see *Back to Bataan.* The Madison had *Practically Yours,* with Claudette Colbert and Fred MacMurray. All the theaters had double features.

Downtown theaters and stores gained more revenues after the war ended. (BHC)

Beneath portraits of their father and grandfather, Henry Ford II stands behind brothers, Benson and William Clay. (MV)

Gary Cooper and Loretta Young starred in *Along Came Jones,* and Tom Conway and Rita Corday were the leads in *Falcon in San Francisco.*

The playhouses also were drawing well. Large crowds saw *Tobacco Road,* starring John Barton, at the Shubert on Lafayette, and families gravitated to the Cass to see Olsen & Johnson and Betty Garrett in *Laffing Room Only.*

Stay-at-homes had a choice of six major radio stations to listen to: WJR, CKLW, WWJ, WXYZ, WJLB, and WJBK. Older foreign-born Detroiters leaned to WJLB to hear music and language from the old country. The station had a Greek Hour, Italian Hour, Polish Hour, Ukranian Hour, and other ethnic programs. Sports addicts tuned to WXYZ and "The Sports Parade" with Don Wattrick, Monday through Friday at 7 p.m.

Theaters did better after the Jack Benny Program concluded its Sunday half hour at 7:30 p.m. The show remained one of Detroit's favorites for years. A record number of Detroiters tuned in to hear Joe Louis as a guest. The champ seemed at ease sparring lines with Benny.

Since Edsel Ford's death, Harry Bennett, head of Ford Motor Company's thug security force, had Henry Ford's ear regarding management decisions. The result was financial chaos, leading to intervention by Mrs. Henry Ford and Mrs. Edsel Ford. With strong backing from his mother and grandmother, who finally convinced his grandfather of his leadership abilities, Henry Ford II assumed the presidency of the ailing company. Bennett and many executive level members quickly became history.

POSTWAR: 1946-1959

Streetcar fares were raised to 10 cents in 1946, and Detroit had enough phones to have a two-volume directory. A strike against General Motors lasting nearly four months was settled, and within two weeks afterward, Walter Reuther was elected president of the UAW-CIO. The old Willow Run Bomber plant became the new Kaiser-Frazer automobile plant, with more potential union members. With wages and prices inching up, a 1946 Pontiac with all the trimmings cost $1,646.

Three studies were conducted—one each by the state, county, and city—on where to place a new metropolitan airport. The studies agreed that the airport should be at Eight Mile Road and Schaefer. However, city councilman Billy Rogell, who had been the Tigers' shortstop from 1930 through 1939, thought it should be within the confines of Wayne County and fought for its Romulus location.

WWJ-TV, Channel 4, was the sixth television station in the country. When daily experimental programs began on March 4, 1947, Detroit homes accounted for fewer than a hundred televisions. By June 3, when the daily commercial schedule began, it was estimated that the Detroit area had 2,000 TVs.

June 3, 1947, was a beautiful Tuesday and over 17,000 fans paid their way into Briggs Stadium to see the Tigers play the Yankees. There was no estimate on how many watched the first Tigers televised game that sunny afternoon.

Programming was mostly local. NBC offered up to three national shows every night except Saturdays. Teenagers loved "Campus Hoopla," at 8:30 every Friday evening. Set in a campus soda shop with several students and cheerleaders, there were quiz and sports segments, and dancing while the jukebox played. Middle-agers preferred "Kraft Television Theatre" on Wednesdays. The one-hour drama had large casts and elaborate sets in well-written and well-acted plays.

Henry Ford, who helped usher in the automobile age, lived until the television era. Ford died five

Billy Rogell, who played alongside Hall of Famers Charlie Gehringer and Hank Greenberg, became a Detroit city councilman in 1942. (photo courtesy Detroit Tigers)

weeks after WWJ aired the first television program in Michigan on March 4, 1947. The 83-year-old Ford had made his last formal public appearance the previous December when he presented watches to veteran employees of his company.

Ford died of a cerebral hemorrhage shortly before midnight on Monday, April 7, with his wife at his side. Governor Kim Sigler ordered flags on state buildings to fly at half-staff until the funeral on April 10. Dearborn's mayor Orville Hubbard proclaimed 30 days of official mourning, and a large portrait of Ford was draped in black and displayed in front of Detroit's city hall for 30 days.

Another familiar face was gone from the Detroit scene. Walter O. Briggs thought Hank Greenberg wasn't worth his salary anymore and sold the slugger to Pittsburgh before the 1947 baseball season began. Greenberg hit more home runs in 1947 than any Tigers player.

The Tigers drew their biggest home crowd ever, 58,369, for a doubleheader against the Yankees.

However, season attendance dropped more than 300,000 from the previous year as the club finished second.

There was change in the mayor's office, too. Eugene I. Van Antwerp defeated Detroit's pre- and post-war choice, Edward J. Jeffries, Jr.

Walter Reuther, president of the UAW-CIO since 1946, was in his kitchen on Detroit's northwest side when an assassin lurking outside the window fired. Reuther was hit in the right arm and shoulder and rushed to the hospital, where he recovered. Reuther resumed his post under the watch of union guards, as the assassin was still at large.

After a 17-day strike at Chrysler, the UAW settled for a 13-cent-an-hour raise to $1.55 an hour. At the same time, on May 29, 1948, the UAW and General Motors agreed on a contract providing for wages tied to the cost of living index. With agreements in hand, Detroit produced over 5 million vehicles in 1948, the first time it matched the output of 5.3 million in 1929.

Briggs Stadium had lights for the first time in 1948. (MV)

The Tigers played their first home night game ever on June 15, 1948, before 54,480 awed spectators under 1,458 large, bright bulbs. Belle Isle drew larger crowds in the summer of '48, as it was the first full year the Children's Zoo was open. Nearby baseball diamonds were busy. Belle Isle ballplayers knew the Tigers had four pitchers that year—Ted Gray, Art Houtteman, Hal Newhouser and Billy Pierce—who grew up playing ball on the sandlots of the island.

Detroit's downtown drivers had to carry more change as parking meters were installed on October 9. That same month, WXYZ, Channel 7, became Detroit's second television station. The cameras and crew occupied the top two floors of the Maccabees Building. Dick Osgood hosted the first program on Saturday, October 9, 1948, a variety and chat program. Guests included band leader Paul Whiteman and actress Frances Langford, who were in town for the event. The mayor and governor spoke, as did television execs.

Programming the first day included the World Series game between Cleveland and the Boston Braves and the last two periods of the University of Michigan vs. Notre Dame football game. The next day, George Pierrot, well known for his world adventure travel films at the Detroit Institute of Arts, introduced his first travel films on television. Detroit's third station, WJBK, Channel 2, debuted two weeks later. At the time there were an estimated 9,000 television sets in the Detroit area.

George W. Trendle, who operated Detroit's first theater built to show movies, and who fathered WXYZ radio and its popular long-running national

George W. Trendle, who chose actor Clayton Moore to portray the Lone Ranger on television, checks out the masked man's pistols. (BHC)

Briggs Stadium hosted the All-Star Game in 1951. (BHC)

programs, wanted to bring the Lone Ranger to television. Brace Beemer, whose voice had been linked to the radio masked man since the death of Earle Graser in 1941, wanted to play the starring role on TV. After all, he was an accomplished horseman and marksman, and he had that great deep voice that millions of listeners were used to hearing three times a week. Beemer, though, was 46 at the time and didn't have the fine features of Trendle's number one choice.

Trendle watched numerous cowboy and adventure movies. He liked Clayton Moore's clean-cut looks and versatility and thought that the 35-year-old actor would do well in a white hat and black mask for the small black-and-white TV screen.

It had been about a year since the attempt on the life of Walter Reuther when his brother was shot. Victor Reuther, the union's educational director, survived but lost an eye. While the police were still investigating both shootings, the union was losing

patience and hired its own investigator.

A few months later, UAW members were thrilled as the union and Ford Motor Company agreed to a contract calling for a pension wholly financed by the company.

As the 1940s came to a close, history was made on December 30 when Mary V. Beck was sworn in as the first woman elected to the City Council. There was change at the top, too, as Albert E. Cobo, city treasurer for seven terms, was elected mayor.

According to the United States Bureau of Census, Detroit's 1950 population was 1,849,568, a gain of 246,116 over the previous decade. In those 10 years, the black population doubled and topped 16 percent of the city's 1950 total.

Detroit remembered former mayor John C. Lodge, who died in February at age 87, by naming the newly opened stretch of its north-south expressway in his honor.

In May the United Auto Workers and General Motors announced a five-year contract calling for guaranteed annual wage increases, cost of living adjustments, and a $100 monthly pension at age 65 after 25 years of service. Auto workers were earning $73.25 weekly or $3,809 yearly, while the average major league ballplayer earned $13,228.

Mayor Hazen Pingree had suggested back in 1890 that Detroit should build a civic center on the downtown waterfront. It took until June 11, 1950, for the city to open the first structure—the Veterans Memorial Building.

Detroit celebrated its 250th birthday in 1951 with events, conventions, and parades. Decorative bunting adorned buildings, City Hall, and Briggs Stadium, site of the major league All-Star game on July 10.

A 59-day strike by Detroit Street Railway operators threatened the celebration, but Detroiters overrode the lack of public transportation by offering rides to those waiting at the usual DSR transportation stops. Mothers and children kept their usual doctor or dentist appointments downtown until the strike ended on June 19. It wasn't unusual to see people waiting at the usual stops for an unknown motorist to stop and ask them for their destination.

President Harry Truman spoke to a huge crowd on July 24, and four days later the biggest Detroit

Hudson's unrolled its huge flag, and other stores decorated as well in 1951. (MV)

President Harry Truman spoke to thousands of Detroiters on July 24, 1951. (photo by Harry Wolf)

A parade heads down Woodward in 1951. (photo by Harry Wolf)

Al Kaline won the 1955 American League batting championship when he was 20 years old. (MV)

parade in 250 years took place. When the celebrations became a memory, Detroit had permanent exhibitions as the new Detroit Historical Museum was opened.

The Tigers finished last for the first time in their franchise history, and the Green Hornet finished its last live broadcast in December, 1952. Al Hodge, who played the Green Hornet the first year the program went on the air from the WXYZ studios in 1936, continued in the role for six more years until entering the service in 1942. In 1952 Hodge was playing Captain Video, one of the highest rated television programs in America. Douglas Edwards, who also was with WXYZ radio a decade earlier, was TV's highest rated newscaster on CBS News.

"Howdy Doody," Kate Smith, and Perry Como were the most popular television programs in the country in 1952. Number four came from Detroit's WXYZ studios and was called "Auntie Dee." Dee Parker's children's program was the only locally produced program in TV's top ten.

Detroit boys liked a local WXYZ-TV show called "Justice Colt." J.D. Beemer, whose father Brace still was the voice of the Lone Ranger on radio, introduced cowboy movies and gave commentary as Justice Colt.

The Red Wings were Detroit's big winners as they took hockey's Stanley Cup. Future owner Mike Ilitch, who turned 23 on July 20, 1952, was playing shortstop in the Tigers' minor league chain.

All major league teams except the Tigers had at least one black player on their team or in their minor league system in 1953. When Claude Agee signed a minor league contract in August 1953, the Tigers became the last major league team to sign a black player.

After 2,956 radio episodes, the Lone Ranger did its last live broadcast from the WXYZ studios on East Jefferson on September 3, 1954. Brace Beemer, the voice of the masked man since the death of Earle Graser in 1941, became the voice of Sergeant Preston in its last live broadcast season.

Northland Center, called the largest regional shopping mall in the country, opened in 1954. At the time, the Detroit Board of Commerce estimated the city's population had reached 2 million.

Eight years earlier, General Motors, Chrysler, Ford, Crosley, Hudson, Kaiser-Frazier, Nash, Packard, and Studebaker all had their assembly lines humming. By 1954 only two of the smaller six companies remained beside the Big Three, as Hudson and Nash formed American Motors and Packard and Studebaker merged.

On April 12, 1955, the Mariners Church building was moved 880 feet to its present location on the south side of Jefferson after four months of preparation. It took 27 months of construction for the City County Building to reach completion. On September 23, 1955, Mayor Cobo led a procession of city officials from the old City Hall down Woodward to their new governmental home as the second building in the civic center was opened.

Motorists were moving faster as the interchange linking the John C. Lodge and Edsel Ford Expressways opened. Al Kaline won the 1955 American League batting championship at the age of 20, and the following year, ownership of the Tigers passed from the Briggs family to a syndicate headed by John Fetzer.

Streetcars were history in 1956 as the Detroit Street Railway became completely motorized. The Woodward line was the last operating in 1955, and thousands turned out to witness Detroit's last streetcar screeching to a permanent halt on April 7, 1956. Mexico City offered more than a million dollars for 184 of Detroit's streetcars.

The Greyhound station, built on the west side of Washington Boulevard at Grand River in 1937, featured a busy Cunningham's Drug Store in the 1940s and 1950s. (MV)

While Studebaker Corporation closed the Packard plant on the east side, a gift by the Ford Motor Company and the Ford and Mercury dealers of America helped open the Henry and Edsel Ford Auditorium at the foot of Woodward. The 2,926-seat auditorium was the new home of the Detroit Symphony Orchestra and also gained national recognition when Ed Sullivan brought his one-hour variety show, "Toast of the Town," to Detroit for one Sunday night that year.

The Ford Motor Company sold its common stock to the public for the first time in 1956 and Detroit had the country's first Black owned and operated radio station, WCHB. The growing Wayne University became a state university in 1956 and dated its founding from 1868, when the School of Medicine opened.

John Todd, the radio voice of Tonto on the Lone Ranger for 24 years, died at the age of 80 in 1957. Todd played in musicals and stock companies before joining the Marines during World War I, and he had appeared on Broadway before joining WXYZ in 1933. While doing radio roles on the Lone Ranger, Green Hornet and Sergeant Preston, Todd taught drama for 16 years at the Detroit Conservatory of Music. He had enjoyed being part of comedy routines on "The Soupy Sales Show," which aired at 11 p.m.

"Lunch With Soupy Sales," was billed as a children's television show but adults loved it also. Also popular with Detroit's adult television watchers in the afternoon were George Pierrot and Bill Kennedy. Both hosts simply sat and chatted—Pierrot with a guest who showed and narrated a travel film, and Kennedy about the feature film and the actors in it. Kennedy, who became a local TV movie host in 1952, had some bit parts in Hollywood movies in the 1940s and turned up in a couple of early television Lone Ranger episodes as the bad guy. He wisely gave up a non-lucrative acting career for a continuing role every week day afternoon in Detroit.

Detroit had a fourth major league franchise as the Fort Wayne Pistons basketball team became the Detroit Pistons and moved into Olympia Stadium.

Detroit also gained Zollner Pistons, an automotive supply company, which produced 70 percent of all pistons used by America's truck manufacturers. Owner Fred Zollner thought Detroit would produce more revenue for both businesses.

Eastland Shopping Center opened in 1957, the same year Jimmy Hoffa became the boss of the Teamsters Union. Albert E. Cobo was the first mayor of Detroit to die in office. City council president Louis C. Miriani was appointed mayor on September 14 and was elected to that position on November 5. The election provided a historic note as Mary V. Beck became the first woman president on the City Council after becoming the first woman to sit on the council eight years earlier.

In 1959, while 16-year-old Aretha Franklin was belting out gospel tunes at her father's New Bethel Church in west Detroit, Barry Gordy borrowed $800 from his parents to start a record company in a house on West Grand Boulevard. Gordy's venture would later become Motown Records.

Kern's Department Store on Woodward south of Hudson's disbanded in 1959 and the new headquarters of the National Bank of Detroit went up at Woodward and Fort, where Detroit's first skyscraper, the Hammond Building, had opened 60 years earlier.

While the Tigers had come up with a black player of Dominican origin the year before in Ozzie Virgil, Larry Doby became the first African-American player on the Tigers in 1959—the same year Detroit police patrol cars were racially integrated for the first time.

While black families were moving to Detroit, industry and white families were moving out. For the first time in the century, Detroit's population declined from the previous decade. The 9.6 percent decline left 1,670,144 Detroiters, included 482,229 black residents, who now made up 28 percent of Detroit's population.

Detroit's beer wars claimed a casualty as Van Patrick, long associated with Goebel beer on Tigers broadcasts, was dropped by Stroh's, the new sponsor for the 1960 season. Stroh's new play-by-play man was Ernie Harwell, previously on the Baltimore Orioles' broadcast team.

THE 1960s

In addition to following their favorite sports teams, Detroiters followed news and newsmakers, and Detroit TV news announcers became local celebrities. Jac LeGoff of WJBK, Channel 2, was the most popular. Many viewers switched to WWJ, Channel 4, to see witty Sonny Eliot do a fun weather report. Newly arrived sportscaster Dave Diles gained a large following on WXYZ, Channel 7's low-rated news team.

Cobo Hall, Detroit's large exhibition hall named for Mayor Albert E. Cobo who had died in office three years earlier, was officially opened in August

Billboards advertised a 1961 Chrysler for $2,964. (photo by Harry Wolf)

by Mayor Louis Miriani.

An estimated 60,000 people crowded into the Campus Martius area on a sunny Labor Day to hear Democratic hopeful John F. Kennedy speak in front of old City Hall. In October, thousands lined both sides of Woodward to see President Dwight D. Eisenhower stand up and wave from a slow-moving opentop limousine, hoping to convince Detroiters to vote the Republican ticket in November.

On November 6, the *Detroit Times* ceased publication and was bought by the *Detroit News,* which raised its price by a penny to eight cents.

The empty Old City Hall waits for the wrecking ball in June 1961. (photo by Harry Wolf)

Demolition is under way in September 1961. (photo by Harry Wolf)

Briggs Stadium was officially renamed Tiger Stadium in 1961, and the Nederlander family opened the lavish Fisher Theatre. The huge new post office opened at Fort and Eighth, and Diana Ross bought a two-flat home for her family on Buena Vista, two houses off Dexter. Robert S. McNamara resigned as president of the Ford Motor Company to become Secretary of Defense.

By October 1961, nothing remained of the old City Hall as bulldozers leveled the area across Michigan Avenue from where the Majestic Building was being demolished. Across Woodward, 30-year-old Joseph L. Hudson was named chief executive officer of Hudson's Department Store.

WXYZ commentator Lou Gordon was no fan of Mayor Louis Miriani, and audiences picked up on that quickly during Gordon's nightly five-minute radio commentary program following the evening news. Gordon was elated in November when 33-year-old attorney Jerome P. Cavanaugh scored a stunning upset over Miriani to win a four-year term as Detroit's chief executive. Cavanaugh, who lived on Wisconsin in the Six Mile-Wyoming area, now could afford a larger home, as the mayor of Detroit earned $25,000 a year.

Mayor Cavanaugh appointed Alfred Pelham to become city controller. It was the highest position in city government next to mayor, and Pelham became the first black man ever even named to a major post in Detroit. Pelham clearly was the best choice as he had served as county budget director and taught at Wayne State University. To help city fi-

The Ford Rotunda was built in 1936 and was destroyed by fire on November 9, 1962. The sprawling Rouge Plant is in the background. (MV)

nances, Cavanaugh pushed for a 1 percent city income tax, which was approved.

Later in the year, on November 9, 1962, fire destroyed the Ford Rotunda. It had stood for 26 years and in the 1950s it was ranked the fifth most popular attraction with tourists.

Detroit lost two live theaters in 1963 as the Shubert-Lafayette on Lafayette and Shelby was razed to became a parking lot, and the Cass, at Lafayette and Washington Boulevard, was operating as a movie house.

While downtown's show palaces were undergoing changes, the Michigan Consolidated Gas Company Building at Woodward and Jefferson opened, as did the 28-story Detroit Bank & Trust Company Building at the southeast corner of Fort and Washington Boulevard.

Edward Davis became the first African American to open a Chrysler dealership. Davis operated a Studebaker franchise from 1940 to 1956 when the automaker went bankrupt, then turned his attention to selling used cars. At the time Davis opened his Chrysler dealership on Dexter, General Motors and Ford franchises were still all white owned.

On Sunday, June 23, 1963, an estimated 125,000 people participated in a civil rights march led by Dr. Martin Luther King. Many linked arms as they marched down Woodward from Adelaide Street to Cobo Hall. The sound of thousands of voices singing "We Shall Overcome" and "The Battle Hymn of the Republic" carried for blocks.

Lending support to Dr. King were Mayor Jerome P. Cavanaugh, former governor John P. Swainson, Police Commissioner George Edwards, and Walter Reuther. Dr. King proclaimed that the Detroit demonstration for civil rights was the "largest and greatest ever held in the United States."

President John F. Kennedy was assassinated in Dallas, Texas, on November 22, 1963. When the official announcement of his death came Friday afternoon, Detroit's city and county government began sending employees home, readying for a complete shutdown to mourn with the nation. Saddened Detroiters walked slowly to their cars, and motor-ists left the downtown area driving slowly, eyes on the road and radios tuned to the sad reports from Dallas.

The news affected scheduled and group activities. The Saturday college football games in Ann Arbor and Lansing were canceled. The Red Wings Sunday game at Boston was called off, as was the Pistons home game at Cobo Arena. The National Football League announced its Sunday games, including the Lions at Minnesota, would go on as scheduled, but all radio and television coverage would be canceled.

Local and national radio and television stations canceled all entertainment programs and carried only special news and memorials without commercial advertising until after the Monday funeral.

The Fisher Theater canceled *Hello Dolly!* starring Carol Channing, through Monday evening. The United Artists lost a lot of revenue as it canceled its showing of *Cleopatra,* starring Elizabeth Taylor, and the CineramaMusic Hall canceled *How the West Was Won.* The Grand Circus canceled *Take Her She's Mine,* starring Sandra Dee and Jimmy Stewart, and the Michigan canceled *Palm Springs Weekend,* starring Troy Donohue, Connie Stevens, and Stefanie Powers. All of the downtown movie houses soon followed with closing announcements until after the Monday funeral.

The day after the funeral, Mayor Cavanaugh proposed naming the old City Hall site for the late President.

The 30-story apartment building at 1300 Lafayette was built in 1964, and acreage east of it was cleared to make way for Elmwood Park. A short drive away, the Goebel Beer brewery shut down after 91 years in Detroit. Lagging sales put Goebel far behind its next door neighbor, Stroh's. The loss of Goebel meant the loss of Brewster the Goebel Rooster, the popular cartoon character used in television commercials.

Early in 1965, Brace Beemer chatted about his days on WXYZ radio doing the Lone Ranger with WJR's early morning personality J.P. McCarthy. Beemer also guested with Detroit TV host Bill

Kennedy. A few days later, on March 7, the 62-year-old Beemer was playing cards with friends at his farm in Oxford and suffered a fatal heart attack. McCarthy broadcast a memorial to Beemer by rounding all those who were still living and had been associated with the Lone Ranger program.

Ratings showed McCarthy was number one in his early morning radio time slot on WJR, and WJR stayed in first place until 3 p.m. Number one belonged to WKNR from 3 p.m. to midnight.

Bearing an imposing dark granite facing, the 23-story twin-towered First Federal Savings & Loan Association Building at Woodward and Michigan opened in August. The first major hotel built in Detroit in 38 years, the 25-story Hotel Pontchartrain, was completed on Jefferson and Washington Boulevard, and the giant model of the Garland Stove was moved from East Jefferson to the State Fairgrounds on Woodward.

Due to his implementation of affirmative action and urban renewal programs, and for lowering property taxes, 38-year-old Jerome P. Cavanaugh was re-elected mayor in November 1965.

The last commercial airlines left Willow Run Airport in 1966, and all airlines were operating from Metropolitan Airport. The Kern store—out of business for seven years—became a memory as the store and surrounding block at Woodward and Campus Martius were razed

Sales for the 67-year-old Kresge Company topped $1 billion for the first time, and founder Sebastian S. Kresge died at 99. In 1966, a hundred years after James Vernor sold his first ginger ale, the Vernor family sold the ginger ale company bearing their name to a national bottling company.

On Sunday, July 23, 1967, at 3:50 a.m., police raided an after-hours drinking spot and arrested 73. About an hour later when police were leaving with

Buildings on the Kern's block were razed in 1966. (BHC)

the last of those arrested, bottles and rocks began flying from a crowd gathered across the street.

The crowd surged down Twelfth Street hurling objects, and by 6:30 a.m. the first fire destroyed a sacked shoe store as rioters didn't allow arriving firemen to put out the blaze. An all-black firefighting force was quickly put together in the hope they wouldn't be harassed and would be allowed to put out fires. It didn't work as they were also pelted with bottles, bricks, rocks, and cans.

Bullhorn pleas by John Conyers, Rev. Nicholas Hood, and other community leaders weren't accepted and they were also forced into retreat.

Newspapers and radio and television stations honored a request by Damon Keith, at the time co-chairman of the Michigan Civil Rights Commission, for a blackout of the events unfolding on Twelfth Street. Businesses shut down on Monday and instructed their employees to stay home, and most streets were empty except for army vehicles. Governor Romney ordered 1,500 National Guardsmen into the city and President Johnson sent 4,700 Army paratroopers.

Three thousand arrests were made on Wednesday, July 26. By the time the disturbance ended, 7,331 had been arrested. The incarcerated were kept in local, county, and state jails, city buses, police garages and gymnasiums, and in the Belle Isle public bathhouse.

The riot resulted in over 1,300 fires, 2,700 looted businesses, 347 injuries and 43 killed. Thirty-three of the dead were black, and blacks accounted for most of the homeless. Many of the families whose homes were burned were housed in Fort Wayne.

By the end of July, the new Detroit Committee was formed by the mayor and governor. Henry Ford II became an active participant and announced that 5,000 workers would be hired from the black neighborhoods without written job tests. Ford also would provide bus transportation to take workers to and from the plants.

While blacks made up close to 40 percent of the city's population and 55 percent of the public school enrollment in 1967, only five percent of Detroit's police force was black. However, by March 1968, Detroit had increased the pay of its police officers to $10,000 per year, the highest in the country.

Lou Gordon quit his WXYZ commentary program, deciding instead to host his popular, hard-hitting interview program on Channel 50.

While Detroit confronted its problems in 1968, the Tigers provided a pleasant diversion by winning more baseball games than any other major league team. At 4:46 p.m. on October 10, 1968, in St. Louis, catcher Bill Freehan caught the last out of the World Series, giving the Tigers the World Championship.

A tremendous celebration began in Detroit. Confetti rained from skyscrapers, horns blared, and people poured from buildings ready to party. Blacks embraced whites and whites embraced blacks as the Tigers helped bring Detroiters together, but after the celebration ended, whites still were moving to the suburbs in increasing numbers.

Masco, founded by Alex Manoogian in 1924, was listed on the New York Stock Exchange for the first time in 1969, and Hudson's merged with the Dayton Corporation, based in Minneapolis.

DARK TIMES: 1970-1989

The Detroit of 1970 had 1,514,063 people, according to the highest figure published by the United States Census Bureau. This figure was smaller than the city's 1930 population, and represented an estimated loss of nearly half a million since its peak of about 2 million in 1954. Over 660,000 black people lived in Detroit in 1970 and accounted for close to 44 percent of the city's residents.

Whites and blacks came together to help former heavyweight champion Joe Louis ease his financial burden. A dinner was held to help the ailing hero, who owed the Internal Revenue Service and had racked up medical bills due to physical and mental problems. Louis was unable to attend, however, as his mental condition was deteriorating.

Walter Reuther, who had fought for so many years to improve working conditions for auto workers through the UAW, died in a small plane crash that year. 1970 also saw the opening of First Independence National Bank, the first African-American owned and operated bank in the country.

The police force, which was only 5 percent black when the '67 riots broke out, was 15 percent black by 1971. The goal of Mayor Roman S. Gribbs was to increase the percentage of black officers on the police force to a percentage equal to the black segment of Detroit's population.

James F. (Prophet) Jones, who lived in a 54-room graystone chateau at 75 Arden Park, died at the age of 63. The African-American preacher's church on Linwood was a popular destination for followers who lavished expensive gifts on him. Jones had 12 servants, five Cadillacs, 400 suits, and a long white mink coat at his disposal.

The *Free Press* raised its price by a nickel from ten to fifteen cents in 1971, and Gordie Howe played his final game as a Red Wing on April 4 that year.

George W. Trendle, who gave WXYZ radio its name and a long string of hit radio serials while operating many downtown movie theaters, died in 1972 at the age of 87.

Founded in 1899, Kresge moved its headquarters from Detroit to Troy and Pfieffer Beer, brewed in Detroit for 83 years, went out of business.

On May 22, 1972, Henry Ford II announced at the Economic Club of Detroit that the riverfront development that would later evolve into Renaissance Center would begin soon.

Detroit had been tossing around a riverfront stadium idea as the city bid on the 1968 and 1972 Olympics. When the Olympics went elsewhere, Detroit proposed a domed stadium on the riverfront west of Cobo Hall that would seat 70,000 for football and 55,000 for baseball. While Henry Ford II had grand plans for the riverfront just east of the Windsor Tunnel, his brother, William Clay Ford, wasn't happy with the traffic patterns of a riverfront stadium and decided a Pontiac location would better serve the interests of Lions fans. When Pontiac voters opted in December 1972 to fund construction on a domed stadium, it meant sudden death for Detroit's stadium hopes.

Left: Flash bulbs pop as Todd Jones strikes out Carlos Beltran on a low curve for the last play at Tiger Stadium. (MV)

Below: The last game is over and the ceremonies end as the fans take a final look at the field. (IC)

I realized we would be sitting behind the area my favorite player would patrol.

It took a while to get acclimated as it was the first time I had seen the infield. The tarp had covered the area on my previous two visits. I was surprised to see grass in the infield, as I had expected a dirt infield like the school baseball diamond.

I also expected play-by-play man Harry Heilmann to announce the game over the loudspeaker. But by the time Hoot Evers lined a double past the outstreched glove of leftfielder Gus Zernial (whose name is the answer to the trivia question, "Who introduced Joe DiMaggio to Marilyn Monroe?"), I was able to follow the game intently.

In August 1951 I went to my first night game at Briggs Stadium. We sat down the first base line and had a good view of Joe DiMaggio popping up to infielder Neil Berry to end the game.

1952 was a sad time for me as the Tigers traded Evers, along with George Kell, Johnny Lipon, and Dizzy Trout, to the Boston Red Sox. My father understood and took me to the center field bleachers the next time Boston came to town.

I saw the legendary Satchel Paige baffle the Tigers with an assortment of pitches in 1953, and I watched as Ted Williams hit four home runs in a high-scoring doubleheader in 1954. 1955 belonged to young Al Kaline and I was there when Kaline hit two home runs in one inning that Sunday afternoon as the Tigers blew Kansas City away 16-0.

Fast forward to Kaline's last year as a player in 1974. It was my first year as a baseball writer/photographer working for a baseball monthly, and Kaline was the first player I ever interviewed.

Besides getting to know the ballplayers, I got to know the old ballpark better as I was granted field,

THE FINAL GAME
at the Corner
September 27, 1999
Detroit vs. Kansas City

The beginning of the last game. (MV)

clubhouse, and press box privileges. I got to know the people working behind the scenes and in the front office, and I went to work for the Tigers after the 1983 season as Director of Group Ticket Sales.

The maintenance guys took a big old brown desk and chair out of the storage room and dusted it off for me. Decades ago, former club owner Frank Navin had used the same furniture for years.

1984 was the stadium's best year attendance-wise, and my first full season culminated with a World Series ring. Few had the opportunity to get to know the old ballpark as a longtime fan, writer, photographer, and member of the front office.

1985 topped everything as I was asked to confirm every seat and bleacher space in the storied stadium. The Tigers were going to a computerized ticket and needed to verify each section against an existing schematic. With clipboard in hand, I viewed the field from every row in the upper and lower decks. I discovered a box seat in the lower visitors' bullpen area and six upper reserved seats the schematics didn't list.

There were other highlights. The lows came later. The end arrived abruptly in August 1992, when a Detroit-headquartered pizza baron came up with the dough to buy out an Ann Arbor-based pizza baron.

As one interested in the rebirth of Detroit, I attended the groundbreaking of the new ballpark and followed its construction with camera and interest as the final games wound down in Tiger Stadium.

Closing day was as good as it gets. Great weather. Great game. Great memories. More than a century of baseball at Michigan and Trumbull ended. A half century of memories ended for me. I experienced it as only a lucky few did.

Souvenir stand outside the old ballpark. (IC)

2000: COMERICA PARK

Opening day. New ballpark. New century. Cold and damp.

I went to the top row of the upper deck, where I had a better view of years and years of memories. The memories, of course, were from the neighboring buildings, not from the field far below on this baseball inaugural.

The red, box-like building on Madison, just west of the Detroit Athletic Club, behind right center backing up to Adams, was where I had worked in 1960. I was an office boy that summer, working out of the mail room in the rear of the third floor. The view back then would overlook today's infield. In 1960 I had a great view of the YMCA and Wolverine Hotel.

While the opening day ballgame was unfolding into part of Detroit's history, I kept perusing the skyline and the memories kept coming. The closest tall building to the right field foul pole was the David Broderick Building. My dentist had been on the seventh floor. As a 12-year-old I was allowed to take the DSR Dexter bus downtown for appointments. Friends came along to experience the view and downtown.

Just east on Witherell was the Madison Theater Building where the Lone Ranger idea was born. Crossing Broadway, the elegant theater that evolved into the Detroit Opera House was in a former life the Broadway Capitol. My father often took me there

on Sunday afternoon for Roy Rogers and Abbott & Costello movies before Detroit had its 250th birthday.

I could see the area where comedians Bud Abbott and Lou Costello gave their first performance ever as a team, after a mediocre career as separate acts on the vaudeville circuit.

Who's on first?

Even from the top row of the upper deck way down the third base line, Tony Clark loomed larger than I thought. The seats aren't as far from the action as I expected. By the end of the third inning, I had circled Comerica Park three times on all levels except the suite level.

I continue exploring. I don't feel bad about missing each pitch, as the VCR at home is capturing the game. Besides, it's not fun to sit in a wet, cold. seat exposed to the elements on this historic day for Detroit. The luxury box suites are the place to be in this weather.

Luxury box users have private parking, a private club, a private entrance, and private bathrooms. They don't have to rub elbows with the unmoneyed taxpayer who helped pay for this project.

Fans, though, should go to Comerica Bank for some cash to cover the increased parking, ticket, and concession prices, before coming to Comerica Park for a ballgame this century.

Right: In 1909 the YMCA building stood on the site where Comerica Park is now located. (BHC)

Below: Looking east on Adams from Witherell in 1907 before the YMCA was erected on the corner. (BHC)

While the 1935 World Champion Tigers played at Navin Field, this is how the future Comerica Park site looked. The YMCA is at the corner of Adams and Witherell. The large building is the Wolverine Hotel on the northwest side of Witherell and Elizabeth. (from the Manning Brothers Historic Photographic Collection)

The project's construction workers unfurl a 150-by-300-foot flag for the National Anthem on opening day. (IC)

The view from the top row on a cold, damp opening day. (IC)

The historic first pitch from Brian Moehler was a fastball that Seattle's Mark McLemore took for a strike. (IC)

The new century brought a new ballpark and new hope to downtown. (MV)

2001 Comerica Park

The Tigers lost too many games and attendance plummeted.

Top executives bailed out during the season and owner Mike Ilitch tried to fill the void by naming Al Kaline as a top advisor.

Before Kaline could advise him, however, the media reported that Ilitch claimed he wasn't aware of the outfield dimensions while the ballpark was becoming a reality and he also was unaware of the ticket price structure until it was announced.

Fans didn't buy it and didn't buy enough tickets, either. While Ilitch is paying high prices for advisors, here's some free advice for Mr. I:

• Cut parking prices in half at all of your lots. Fans feel ripped off the moment they drive up.

• Cut concession prices.

• Cut the outfield dimensions in left center field by putting the bullpens in front of the present wall.

• Cover the present right field bullpens with affordable bleacher spaces.

The ballpark will feel cozier and more seats will be filled with fans.

Putting bleachers over the bullpen area would give the ballpark a cozier feel. (IC)

The Tiger carousel in the center of the food court is a popular attraction for families. (IC)

The stainless steel statue of Al Kaline may catch a home run before the century is over. (IC)

CAMPUS MARTIUS

By the 1990s, downtown Detroit had attained international fame as the world's largest collection of abandoned buildings, with a slice of life here and there in Greektown and Foxtown.

The new century finally brought hope. For the first time in decades, downtown Detroit shows promise and projects. Even though Detroit's population may never top 1 million again, the downtown area could become the most upscale neighborhood in the metro region.

Old buildings renovated into lofts for housing, along with Brush Park's new housing, are giving downtown more residents. Activities at Comerica Park, Ford Field, and Harmonie Park all help, but not enough to resuscitate the heart of the business district.

Having General Motors take over the Renaissance Center as its world headquarters was great news for the city, but the buildings had tenants before GM. The biggest downtown development project so far this century began on April 12, 2000, when Compuware broke ground for its new headquarters near the former site of the J.L. Hudson building. The software company will anchor Campus Martius and its neighboring development, giving downtown a heartbeat and economic base after decades of embarassing emptiness.

The photos on the cover and these pages provide a retrospective of Campus Martius—yesterday and today.

Architect's drawing of the new Compuware Headquarters that will anchor the emerging Campus Martius development. (illustration courtesy of Rosetti Associates)

1862 street scene in Campus Martius. (MV)

Horses and buggies meet automobiles and streetcars around Campus Martius in 1915. (BHC)

In 1937 the Detroit Opera House was remodeled into Sam's Department Store. (HW)

Kern's and Hudson's department stores loomed behind Campus Martius. (HW)

Aerial view of Campus Martius and surrounding area in 1960. (HW)

Looking up Woodward at the same area 40 years later as site preparation for the Compuware and Kern Woodward projects is under way. (IC)

Compuware headquarters under construction. (IC)

Kern Woodward Associates is overseeing the development of the Campus Martius area. (IC)

Looking north over Comerica Park to Brush Park and the Medical Center. (IC)

New housing near Comerica Park brings life to downtown. (IC)

ECHOES OF DETROIT

Billy Rogell

Tigers shortstop of the 1930s who became a Detroit city councilman

I saw Detroit when I broke in the with the Boston Red Sox in 1925. It was such a friendly city and I knew right away that I wanted to be traded there. Detroit was booming then in the last years of the 1920s. Every time I came in with the Red Sox, I saw new construction as most of the skyscrapers went up in those few years.

Sonny Eliot

Longtime weatherman who brightened up our days for decades

My father had a hardware store on Hastings and Farnsworth, and we lived nearby. When my mother went to work in the store, my babysitter was the Warfield Theater right near the store. My mother simply took me to the movies and sat me in the theater seat and went to the store. When the movies ended, she came back for me. I could talk before movies could, that's how long ago it was. Of course, downtown was the most exciting place in the world for a kid to go. The people, traffic, and stores were fascinating. I especially loved going to Hudson's toy department.

Eugene Miller

Chairman, Comerica Bank

We would always go very early to the Thanksgiving Day parade to get a good view. That was an important day and important part of our lives. The ballpark was another important part. We lived near Grand River, Joy Road, and West Grand Boulevard. Many times we would just walk to the ballpark. The fondest memory I have was the 1945 World Series when my dad took me to my first ballgame to see the Tigers and the Cubs. This became a ritual for us, to go to a game and walk down Michigan to Lafayette Coney Island and take the streetcar back home.